The Pony Club
Stoneleigh Park
Kenilworth
Warwickshire
CV8 2RW

Website: www.pcuk.org

The Pony Club Guide to Caring for a Horse or Pony
is published by The Pony Club

British Library Cataloguing in Publication Data.
A catalogue record for this book is available from the British Library.

ISBN 978-1-907279-24-9

Design and Production: Paul G. Harding
www.hardingbooks.com

The presence of brand names and logos in the photographs of this book
does not in any way imply endorsement by The Pony Club.

Thanks to the Mark Todd Collection and Jumpers Horse Line
for help with rugs for photography.

Printed by Halstan Printing Group in Amersham, UK
www.halstan.co.uk

Trade distribution by Kenilworth Press
An imprint of Quiller Publishing Ltd.
Wykey House, Wykey, Shrewsbury, SY4 1JA
Tel: 01939 261616 Fax: 01939 261606
Email: info@quillerbooks.com
Website: www.kenilworthpress.co.uk

The Pony Club Guide to

Caring for a Horse or Pony

by Carolyn Henderson
with photographs by John Henderson

Contents

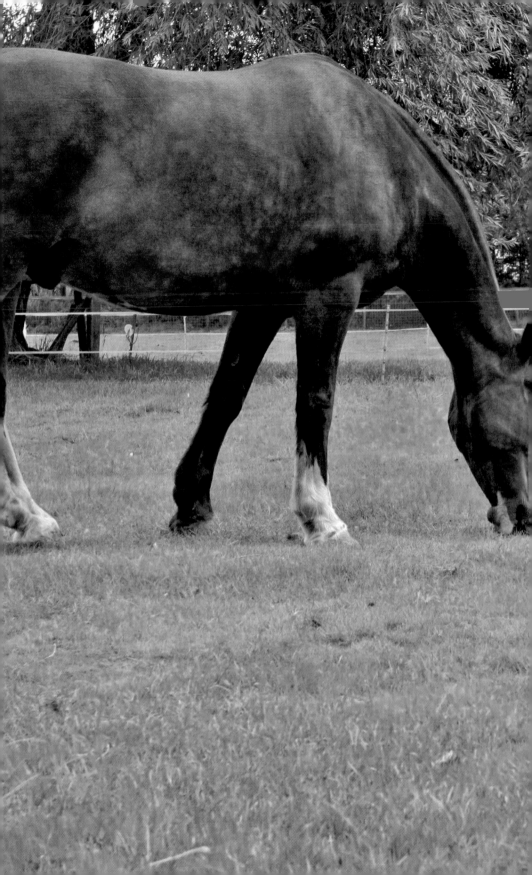

1. Basic Considerations

Looking after a horse or pony is hugely rewarding. It's also a great responsibility, as he depends on you to safeguard his health, safety and general well-being.

If you are a first-time owner or carer, you may feel daunted at how much there is to learn—but everyone has to take that first step. As you progress, you'll find that you never stop learning and that always wanting to find out more is part of the fascination of keeping horses. If you are an experienced owner, it's always good to review the way you do things.

Being a Member of The Pony Club provides you with a wonderful back-up of help and support. Never be afraid to ask your instructors and Branch or centre Officials for advice—and there is lots of information available on The Pony Club website and in specialist Pony Club publications.

Learning to Care

You need a certain level of skill and understanding before you can start looking after a pony. This book will help you, but you also need practical experience, which is where lessons, watching and talking to knowledgeable owners and practical sessions at Pony Club rallies are valuable.

Ensure that whoever will be paying the costs involved realises how much to budget for. Another Pony Club book, *So You Want To Buy*

Family members must be prepared to offer practical help when needed.

a Pony?, will help you decide whether you are ready to take on the responsibility. This isn't meant to put you off, but to underline how important it is to think things through.

Parents must be prepared to offer practical as well as financial help to even the keenest young carers when school or other commitments demand. You don't need to be able to ride to look after a pony, but you must understand how his mind works and be able to handle him safely and correctly. This book will help you to acquire basic skills so that looking after a pony can become a pleasure for all involved.

As parents inevitably have to pay the bills, they must be aware of costs involved. These will vary according to the facilities you opt for, whether you have help or do all the work yourself and even where you live, but if you're a would-be owner weighing up pros and cons, analysing these basic costs will help you budget:

- Rental of stable and grazing and costs of any help given.
- Fuel costs involved in travelling to and from the yard.
- Hay and any extra feed needed.
- Bedding.
- Stable and yard equipment such as buckets, mangers, haynets and mucking out tools if not provided.
- Tack, rugs, grooming kit, first aid kit.
- Routine preventive care: farriery, vaccinations, worming and dental care.
- Lessons so that you and your pony can progress.
- Transport to get to rallies etc.
- Insurance for veterinary fees.

Parents should talk to experienced adults about the back-up help they will need to give so that pony care can be fitted into family and school commitments. This will range from providing transport to helping with daily care—even if that only means walking up a field with a torch on winter evenings to catch and check on a pony!

Transport can add considerable costs to your budget.

Livery Systems

Unless you are lucky enough to own or rent land and facilities, you will keep your horse at livery. This term originates from the time when wealthy landowners supplied their employees with livery—food and clothing—and gradually changed its meaning to cover accommodation and food given to animals. Later still, it evolved to mean yards which provided horses for hire and today's livery yards are horse hotels!

Types of Livery

There are five livery systems: grass, general DIY, part or assisted DIY, full and working.

Grass livery means that a pony lives out all the time, all year round. In one way, it is the most natural way of keeping a horse, but you must have a stable available for emergencies, such as when a pony is ill or injured. As explained later in this book, you will also need strategies in place to make sure he does not become overweight, as this can lead to serious health problems.

If you keep a pony at grass livery on a livery yard or at a riding school, the landowner will be responsible for ensuring that the land is kept in good condition, the fencing is safe and the pony has adequate shelter. Some owners rent grazing and maintain it themselves or pay a contractor to do so, but this involves extra work and costs.

General DIY livery is the most popular form and, if you develop a good working system, is cost effective. It means that you rent a stable and grazing and are totally responsible for your pony's welfare. However, on most yards you will find other owners who can help you when needed in exchange for you returning the favour. As long as arrangements are clear and both parties are conscientious and reliable, this can work well.

Part or assisted DIY livery means that the yard owner/staff help look after your pony. The extra costs will vary according to how much work is involved, but this system can provide your pony with a reliable routine and give you peace of mind. If you take time and travelling costs into account, it may also save money.

Full livery is the most expensive, as the yard owner/staff look after your horse and exercise him when necessary. It is an option sometimes taken by adults who work long or irregular hours if it provides the only way they can own a horse, but isn't recommended for young riders. On the right yard, your pony should be well cared for, but you won't have the pleasure of looking after him, nor will you get to know him and forge the bond that is essential if you are to be partners.

Working livery is offered by some riding schools. Here, the school shares your pony and uses him for lessons in return for a reduced livery cost. The advantage is that the pony will get enough exercise but the disadvantages are that you won't have unlimited access to him and he may be ridden by riders of different abilities.

Choosing a Yard

If you are keeping your pony on a livery yard, it is important that you find one where both you and he are happy. Ask Members and Officials at your Pony Club Branch for recommendations. Some Pony Club Centres may offer livery and many yards now have websites where you can find out about facilities and charges.

Choose a yard where you stand a good chance of making friends and finding like-minded owners. Young riders will probably not be happy on a yard where all the other riders are older, and vice versa!

When you find a potential yard, make an appointment to visit and if necessary, take someone more experienced with you. Your impression

Find a yard where you and your horse will be happy.

should be of a well-kept yard with a pleasant atmosphere. Fields should be in good condition with safe fencing and adequate shelter— *see* Chapter 2 for more information.

All yards must have fire control and security measures. Horse theft is relatively rare, but theft of tack and equipment is, sadly, common. It is down to you to protect your horse through measures such as freeze marking and microchipping and to mark tack and equipment with your postcode, but tackrooms should have adequate locks and security systems.

A good yard owner will be used to assessing clients and their needs and it's a good sign if you are asked lots of questions. You should also expect to see a list of yard regulations, as all yards need rules to run smoothly and safely.

Horse Sense

If you're about to look after your first pony or horse, or are a parent or other family member who will help out when necessary, learn what horses need and how they react. You also need basic handling and management skills: this book will help, but books can't replace practical experience.

Parents should find that others with more experience will help, but it's best to find someone you know is knowledgeable as a first source of advice. It's difficult when you're faced with conflicting opinions and advice, even when everyone who offers them is well-meaning.

Think ahead: if you're an owner and family members you might call on to help don't have experience, invite them to your yard so they learn how to be comfortable and safe around horses. Even small ponies can be daunting in terms of size to those who aren't used to them.

Good riding schools and some colleges offer courses aimed at those new to horses. These range from 'own a pony' days to evening classes and can be very useful. Choose a course which includes hands-on experience; many evening classes include practical daytime sessions on a local yard.

Most horses are friendly and if they are suitable for a novice owner/ rider, should be well-behaved. However, the smallest pony can be stronger than an adult if he puts his mind to it and the quietest pony will react according to his instincts if he is frightened or startled. We must never take good behaviour for granted or become complacent, no matter how well we know a horse.

Horses are, by nature, prey animals and if frightened they will run away rather than stand and be aggressive. If a pony habitually kicks or bites, he is not suitable for a novice owner and should be re-trained by an experienced handler who knows the correct and fair way to do it.

All handlers have a responsibility to behave as correctly as they wish their ponies to behave. Remembering these guidelines will help:

- Avoid making sudden movements or loud noises.
- Speak to him before you touch him so he knows you are there.
- Walk quietly towards him. Don't run, because he will think you are chasing him.
- Learn how your body language can influence him. For instance, if you lower your shoulders, approach him slowly and don't stare at him, you won't worry him and may find him easier to catch in the field. But if you want him to move away from you, it will be easier to influence him if you square your shoulders and look him in the eye.
- Be clear, consistent and fair in what you ask a horse to do. If you ride, you will know that the same rules apply. For example, if one day you insist that he stands whilst you open a gate, walks through quietly and stands whilst you close it, but next day allow him to wander to the end of the lead rope and eat, he won't realise what is expected of him.
- If a horse's behaviour makes him difficult to handle—perhaps he is reluctant to pick up his feet, or pulls when being led to the field—get help in re-training him. Horses are happier and more relaxed when they know how to behave, but good behaviour must be taught clearly and kindly.
- The easiest way to avoid accidents such as being knocked over or having your foot trodden on is to be in the right place at the right time. Avoid standing directly in front of a horse unless for a specific reason; never kneel down beside him, but bend down (preferably) or squat so you can move out of the way quickly.
- Use the correct techniques for routine tasks such as picking up his feet and putting on and removing rugs.
- Always wear safe clothing. Anyone loading, lungeing or clipping should wear a securely fastened hard hat and it's also a good idea to wear a hat when turning out and bringing in a pony from the field. Footwear should also give protection. You might be tempted to wear trainers or sandals in hot weather, but stick to sensible boots. It's essential to wear gloves when lungeing or loading and sensible to wear them when turning out or bringing in your horse.

Catching and Turning Out Techniques

Catching and turning out are essential skills. Even horses who are usually good to catch can be cautious or difficult if approached in the wrong way. You also need to know how to turn out a horse safely, or a horse eager to get to his field or join his friends could hurt you accidentally.

Catching

Make life easier by approaching your horse in the field at times other than when you want to ride him. Put on his headcollar, give him a titbit, stand for a few seconds, then quietly remove the headcollar and walk away.

This builds an association between being caught and a pleasurable experience—food! Don't give titbits regularly, as it can encourage a horse to nip, but make catching an exception. It's important to spend time on this strategy if a horse is difficult to catch.

Always approach him in a calm, unhurried way. Horses have 'blind spots' immediately in front and behind, so walk towards him from the side. Offer him a titbit as you put the rope round his neck, then put on his headcollar.

If your horse is turned out in a group and they are all anticipating being brought in for a feed, the only safe way of managing this may be for all horses to be brought in at the same time. Don't risk being kicked or trampled as other horses try to follow yours through the gate—ask for help and ensure you are wearing your hat, gloves and sensible footwear.

Turning Out

There is always the chance that a horse will kick up his heels and gallop off when turned out, so anyone doing this job must be alert and agile.

If a horse pulls or is otherwise badly behaved on the way to his field, spend time improving his manners on the ground, teaching him to stop and start in response to your body language and actions and to respect your space. If necessary, get help in establishing these lessons.

Using a headcollar which applies pressure on the nose or, if you prefer, a bridle and snaffle bit, will give more control. In both cases, you must be able to apply and release the correct amount of pressure at the appropriate time, just as when riding. Don't carry on applying an aid/ signal when the horse has responded correctly, or you will confuse him.

Lead him through the gate and close it. Continue until you are far enough into the field not to get trapped between flying hooves and the gate, then turn the pony round to face the gate. Ask him to stand still for a moment, then take off his headcollar and move away.

Handling Checklist

Anyone helping to look after a pony must be able to:

- Catch him in the field and put on his headcollar.
- Lead him in from the field, tie him up and take off his headcollar.
- Pick out his feet.
- Recognise when he has a loose shoe which needs to be removed.
- Brush him off as appropriate.
- Recognise signs of an emergency injury or illness and know what to do if or when they happen.
- Recognise signs of minor injury and know what to do. (This may mean simply asking an experienced person's advice.)
- Put on and remove rugs.
- Muck out a stable.
- Fill and tie up a haynet and ensure that clean, fresh water is available.

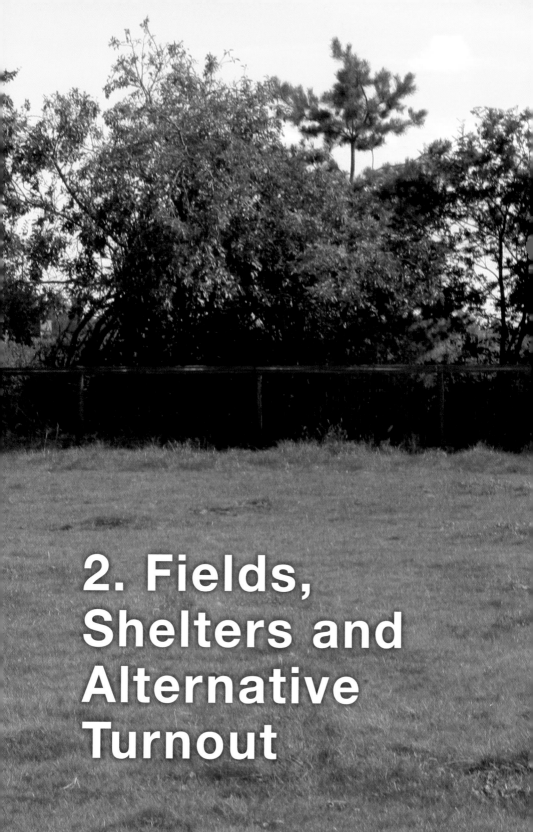

2. Fields, Shelters and Alternative Turnout

Horses are naturally grazing animals and their digestive system is designed to function on a steady intake of forage (grass or hay). In the wild, they spend most of their time eating and will walk as far as necessary in search of suitable food. Domesticated horses have it easy, as we provide grazing for them—and often give them too much of a good thing.

Time in the field is about more than eating. It's a chance for a horse to relax, socialise with his companion(s) and move around, so his field must provide a safe and healthy environment. We now recognise that it is unfair to stable a horse all the time, unless, of course, your vet says he must be on 'box rest' to recuperate from illness or injury.

Field Facts

Things to consider when assessing whether a field is suitable are size and stocking density; land characteristics and type of grass; the presence of poisonous plants—especially ragwort; fencing; shelter; and water supply.

The accepted guideline is that there should be at least one acre (0.4 hectare) per horse, but the type of grazing, the way it is managed and the needs of individual animals must also be taken into account.

For instance, if an animal is overweight or susceptible to laminitis—and the two often go together—you will need to limit grazing as part of a tailored regime and may decide to fence off a smaller area as part of this.

All types of land have pros and cons. There is no such thing as perfect grazing, only perfectly managed land.

For example, clay soil is heavy and becomes waterlogged and rutted. Sandy soil drains well, but ragwort thrives on it. As you'll see later in this chapter, ragwort is poisonous and potentially fatal.

You need to accept the characteristics of the land you use and manage it to make the most of it. Owners of large acreages who have the necessary vehicles and machinery may want to do this themselves, whilst others will find the most efficient and cost-efficient way is to call in a contractor who understands the land characteristics and the needs of horses.

The ideal grazing contains a mix of palatable species, such as fescues and ryegrass. Unfortunately, unless you can start from scratch by sowing a specially formulated grass mix, you may have to use grazing that was

You may need to limit grazing by fencing off a smaller area.

grown for cattle rather than horses. This means that nutrient levels will be too high and you will need to look at ways of limiting intake whilst keeping your pony happy, as explained in Chapter 4 on feeding.

If you can establish new grazing, get advice from a seed specialist who understands horses' needs and the land you propose to use. A specialist can help you make the most of any type of land by suggesting the right mix of grasses and the best sowing density. If your region is liable to long periods without rain, you will need to include more drought-resistant varieties.

Horses will eat plants other than grass and you may be advised to plant herbs. As natural does not always mean good, check that what you are planting is safe—and don't assume that your horse will eat it!

It takes time for grass to establish a good root pattern. If it is grazed as soon as it comes through for the first time, it is more likely that horses will pull it up rather than biting it off.

Poisonous Plants

There are many plants which are poisonous to horses, but the commonest are ragwort, buttercups, bracken, acorns, sycamore seeds, nightshades and yew. As ragwort and buttercups in particular may be found in hay made from poor grazing, it is important that you buy hay from a reputable supplier. Poisonous plants may be difficult to recognise when dried and baled.

Ragwort is a killer. It contains substances which damage a horse's liver and once the damage reaches a certain level, there is no cure and the horse has to be euthanased (put down) to save it from a painful death. It can be fatal even when small amounts are ingested regularly over several years.

Ragwort is biennial, which means it takes two years to complete its cycle of full growth. It forms rosettes in the first year and flowers in the second; the bright yellow flowers are easy to spot, but the rosettes lie close to the ground and are easily missed.

There are two ways of destroying ragwort. One, which works when dealing with small numbers of plants, is to dig it up and pull it out. The other, which may be the only practical method for heavy ragwort infestation and/or maintaining large areas of grazing where plants have been spotted, is to spray it with an appropriate herbicide.

The ragwort plant has a long tap root, so it is easier and more efficient to use a special ragwort fork. Once uprooted, it should be taken away from the field and burned.

Always wear gloves when handling ragwort, as tests have shown that the toxins can be absorbed by people as well as animals.

Yew is so poisonous that a single mouthful can kill. This evergreen tree is traditionally found in churchyards and there have been cases of horses in adjoining fields dying after they have eaten clippings thrown over a fence. You may also find yew trees in woodland, so if you hack in areas where they are known to grow, be careful not to let horses snatch mouthfuls as you pass.

Acorns can cause gastric problems and eventual kidney failure and death. Fallen acorns must be removed. If possible, oak trees and the surrounding area should be fenced off.

Sycamore seeds contain a toxin now known to be linked to a potentially fatal disease called atypical myopathy. They can be carried a long way by air or water and have even been linked to cases where

The commonest plants which are poisonous to horses are (1 and 2) ragwort, (3) buttercups, (4) bracken, (5) acorns, (6) sycamore seeds, (7) nightshades and (8) yew.

fields which have no sycamore trees nearby have been flooded and seeds brought on to them by flood water.

The best strategy is to remove horses from fields containing sycamore seeds in Spring and Autumn, which are the danger times. Think carefully before cutting down trees, as they provide shelter for horses and wildlife.

Buttercups can cause problems if grazed in large quantities, as they may cause inflammation and blisters around the mouth area and/or be implicated in colic (abdominal pain). Heavy growths should be eradicated with a suitable herbicide.

Fencing and Gates

Safe fencing and gates protect horses and people. If a horse escapes because of inadequate or poorly maintained fencing and a road accident results, you could be held responsible and be liable for damages. This is just one reason why every responsible owner should have third party liability cover. This cover is included with Pony Club Membership but you must check that it satisfies your requirements.

Unfortunately, accidents will happen even when fencing is safe and well-maintained, perhaps because a horse crashes into it or kicks out and breaks it. However, you can minimise risks and there are many types of suitable fencing available.

Hedging reinforced by post and rail fencing is a good option.

Thick, well looked-after hedging is generally regarded as the best type of fencing, because it provides shelter as well as acting as a barrier. Modern farming practices means proper hedging—especially that which is cut and laid (a traditional but seldom-seen practice where stems are trimmed and then laid towards the horizontal to give a thick barrier) is becoming rarer.

Thin hedging or a mix of hedges and trees can be reinforced with other types of fencing, usually post and rail or electric, to make it safe and retain the ability to give some shelter.

There are several types of electric fencing, so get advice on which is the best for your needs.

Post and rail fencing is safe and efficient as long as it is high enough to deter horses from jumping out, substantial, and constructed so that the rails can't be pushed off when the horse pushes or rubs himself against them. On softer soils, or if you want extra security, you can add a run of electrified tape or rope offset from the top rail.

Electric fencing can be permanent or temporary. If it must be used as the sole boundary fence, it must be permanent, with substantial wooden posts. Temporary electric fencing, with plastic posts, can be used when it is necessary to divide a securely fenced field into smaller sections. Electrified tape and rope are available, so get specialist advice on which type is best for your situation.

Stock fencing designed especially for horses is useful when you need to keep horses in a field but prevent other animals, such as dogs, from entering. It should be designed so that a horse cannot get a foot caught in the squared wire and there should be no sharp ends on which he could cut himself; sheep or pig fencing is not suitable.

High-tech fencing made from tough but flexible 'plastic' demands minimal maintenance, but is expensive. As materials are developed, new ideas come through, including fencing said to deter insects!

Rabbit fencing may be a useful or even essential back-up to horse fencing in some cases, especially in areas where soil is light and rabbits find it easy to dig burrows. It is set outside field fencing.

Barbed wire fencing can cause terrible injuries and should never be used for horses. Plain wire is less dangerous but not recommended, as there is still a risk of injury. High tensile wire is also potentially dangerous, as it snaps back at high speed when it breaks or is cut.

Field gates must be at least 1.8m wide to allow horses to pass through safely. If you need to get tractors and machinery through, they will need to be wider. Gates must also be well balanced and hung correctly so that they are easy to open and close when leading horses in and out of a field.

Shelter

Horses need shelter and shade all year round. Trees and hedging give a natural solution; the other answer is a purpose-made shelter.

As horses are not agricultural animals, you will probably need planning permission for a permanent shelter, even in rural areas—and some planning authorities are unlikely to grant it. Usually, the answer is to use a mobile field shelter, which should count as a temporary measure even if it is rarely moved. Mobile shelters are built on metal or timber skids and can be towed.

Traditional designs are basically open-fronted stables. Many horses will stand inside a shelter, but others may stand outside and use one of the shelter walls as a windbreak. If this happens, check that the front

Traditional field shelters offer protection in all weathers.

opening is large enough to allow more than one horse through at a time to minimise the risk of a dominant animal bullying others. Shelters with two openings to give an entrance and exit may lessen the risk of one horse trapping or excluding another.

Another design, which some horses prefer and which can also solve bullying problems, is to use a windbreak. This should comprise solid 2-metre wooden sections laid out like the spokes of a wheel.

If your field has any degree of slope, try and site a field shelter on the highest point so water drains away from it and position it so that the back of the shelter faces the prevailing wind. If possible, set it on hard standing.

Water

All horses must have clean water permanently available. Troughs and containers should be large enough to supply all horses in the field and should be strong and safe, with no sharp edges. Old baths are not suitable, as a horse may injure his leg.

If possible, site your water supply away from trees, so that leaves and dirt do not fall in. Keep troughs and containers clean, as many horses will go thirsty and become dehydrated (*see* Chapter 5: Health) rather than drink contaminated water.

You may be lucky enough to have a piped water supply. If not, water must be transported, so the easier the access, the better. In freezing conditions, ice must be broken at least twice a day.

A simple windbreak which is effective and relatively cheap.

25

Field Maintenance

Keeping a field in good condition takes a lot of time and work, but is essential to keep horses safe and to ensure that they get maximum benefit from their grazing.

One of the most important jobs is also the simplest: check your field daily to make sure that fencing is in good repair, that nothing has been thrown or dumped in it that could harm your horse, that there are no poisonous plants which have been missed on previous inspections and that there are no rabbit holes or molehills which could lead to him tripping and injuring himself.

Holes should be filled as soon as you spot them. Moles, like rabbits, are a menace and create soft areas where a horse could trip. It may be necessary to call in a specialist pest controller to deal with either.

It is also vital to remove droppings from the field. This helps prevent the spread of worms—you'll find more information about parasites in Chapter 5. Ideally, remove droppings daily, but if this is impossible, at least weekly. Small fields can be cleared using a wheelbarrow, but a mechanical paddock cleaner may be needed for large acreages. Don't pile droppings at the side of the field, put them on a manure heap.

Some land owners harrow fields with chain harrows to spread droppings instead of removing them. It is sometimes claimed that if this is done in hot weather, UVA rays in sunlight will kill worm eggs. Researchers now say that this is not the case and spreading droppings simply spreads worms.

Perfect Pasture

Grass needs a combination of warmth and moisture to grow: the **ground** temperature, not the **air** temperature, needs to be 5-6 degrees or above, together with sufficient rainfall. The ideal grazing for horses is short and even. Horses are browsers and will graze some areas but not others, so unless you take remedial action, you will end up with lawns and roughs—some areas of short grass and some which grow longer because horses don't graze them. They are also less likely to graze areas where dung is deposited, which is another good reason for removing droppings as often as possible.

It will help if you can take horses off the field for a short time to rest it and, if it is growing well, graze it with sheep or cows. Sheep are sometimes nicknamed 'golden hooves' as they tread down unlevel areas without causing damage. Cows prefer longer grass that horses will leave if the shorter grass they prefer is available.

Just as important, grazing with other species helps reduce the parasite burden. Parasites which live in horses can't survive the digestive systems of other species, nor will they harm them.

Topping—cutting grass to a height of around 5cm (2in)—will encourage it to thicken or 'tiller out' (produce more leaves per stem).

Weed Control

The best defence against undesirable plants such as thistles and nettles is to look after grazing, using the information in this chapter, and establish a thick, dense sward. However, there may be times when you need to use a herbicide (weed killer). It is important to use the right type, as a herbicide which kills one plant may not be effective against others. Nor do you want to apply something which kills a problem plant but also kills your grass!

Some species, such as docks and ragwort, can be spot-sprayed using a backpack spray. Those which manage to get a hold over wide areas, such as chickweed, will probably need widespread application. (Chickweed is not poisonous, but it takes over from grass and most horses won't eat it.)

There are rules and restrictions about the use of herbicide that must be followed to prevent danger to people and animals. These range from rules on who can buy them, to restrictions on their use near water courses.

Whether you are using a herbicide or employing a contractor, check whether horses have to be kept out of the field after any application, and for how long.

Soil Analysis and Fertilising

If you need to fertilise grazing to encourage healthy grass growth, carry out a broad spectrum soil analysis first. You can do this yourself with a soil-testing kit or employ a contractor. Soil samples should be taken from different parts of the field to get an accurate overall picture.

Analysis will establish the levels of elements in the soil and also indicate the level of acidity. In some circumstances, you may only need to measure acidity levels. Acidity levels are measured on a scale and expressed as a number between 1 and 14pH. Ideally, land on which horses are grazed should have a pH level of about 6.5pH. A soil pH that is too low or too high means the availability of minerals and trace elements will be reduced.

In many areas of the UK, soil tends to be too acidic. Traditionally, lime was applied to rebalance it, but it should only be used by or with advice from an expert and horses must be kept off the field until all the lime has been rained in. Some experts advise applying calcified seaweed, which has a similar anti-acidic effect but can be used without removing horses from the field.

Fertilising land for horses is different from fertilising land for other purposes. You need a slow release fertiliser formulated especially for use on horse paddocks, not one with a high level of nitrogen that will prompt an immediate flush of growth and may trigger laminitis.

Repairing Damage

Some damage from horses' hooves is inevitable in wet conditions. The most vulnerable areas are gateways and field shelter sites, so if possible, protect them. Strategies include putting down safe hardcore or using grass mats—special mesh mats which give a firmer base, but allow grass to grow through. Wood chips can be used as a temporary measure, but will soon degrade. Wood chip containing bark degrades faster than clean wood chip and is more likely to become slippery.

Winter Tactics

Try to compensate if there are times when access to fields is restricted— unless, of course, a horse is on box rest through veterinary advice.

Use an outdoor or indoor school as a turnout area. If horses are in there for anything more than a quick leg-stretch, provide forage and water. Clear up discarded forage so it doesn't mix in with the school surface and compromise its properties.

Some yards may have fenced areas of hard standing outside stables or barns so that horses can wander in and out at will. They are still restricted, but it is more natural than keeping them in a stable for long periods.

Feeding in the Field

You'll find information on feeding in Chapter 4, but feeding hay or other forage outdoors is part of both horse care and field care. Make sure that all horses can get their fair share and that dominant animals are not driving others away. This can be a problem when big bales are left out, though compatible animals may share quite happily.

If you put out hay in individual portions, space them out well so that horses don't feel crowded. Always put out more portions than the number of field occupants, so a horse who is driven off by a field bully can move to another helping.

3. Stables, Bedding and Mucking Out

Most owners will choose to stable their horses part of the time and even those whose animals have a 24/7 outdoor lifestyle should ensure that a stable is available should a horse be injured or ill. As with a field, it should provide an environment in which your horse is safe, healthy and happy.

You may hear claims that stables are equivalent to prisons and that all equines should be turned out all the time. When grazing is well managed and when shelter is provided and a horse is happy and stays healthy being kept this way, permanent turnout has a lot to recommend it. However, it doesn't suit all horses and a combined management system is a perfect and sometimes superior alternative.

Many horses relax happily in their stables and want to come in when the weather is bad. Those who show signs of stereotypical behaviour—weaving, wind-sucking and/or crib-biting or box-walking—are stressed by confinement. At one time, these behaviours were called stable vices, which is unfair. They are stress-coping mechanisms.

These behaviour patterns can usually be minimised or prevented by turning a horse out, so common sense suggests that these animals should be kept out permanently, if possible. If it isn't, following recommendations in this chapter and the next one will help.

Many horses, especially those kept on the combined system, will relax happily in their stables.

Internal stables set within a large building require careful attention to ventilation.

Stable Design

There are two sorts of stabling arrangements, external and internal. External stables are individual buildings, though they may be constructed in rows or blocks. Internal stables are constructed within a large building; this set-up is often called an American barn.

Which is best? Internal stabling, with a walkway for access, allows those looking after horses to stay comfortable in all weathers. The disadvantage is that shared airspace allows a more rapid spread of germs and bacteria. It may also be more difficult to ensure good ventilation.

External stables expose carers to the weather, but are easier to ventilate. Depending on the layout of your site, it may also be easier to find a room with a view that a horse will prefer. They, like people, have preferences: some horses like to be able to watch what is going on, but others prefer peace and quiet.

Planning constrictions mean that in most cases, new-build stables will be wooden buildings erected on concrete bases. A base should be laid with a slight slope to aid drainage. Good drainage, whether for internal or external stabling, is important to help minimise a build-up of ammonia, which is detrimental to health.

A stable should be as large as possible. Obviously this gives a horse more room to move, but he is also less likely to kick droppings around. You will have to put more bedding in a large stable to begin with, but in the long run, costs could be relatively smaller because you won't have to remove so much soiled bedding.

Stable doors should be of an appropriate height and open outwards.

Minimum recommended dimensions are 3.7 x 3.05m (12 x 10ft) for a pony up to 14.2hh; 3.7 x 3.7m (12 x 12ft) for a horse up to 16hh; 4.2 x 4.2m (14 x 14ft) for a horse over 16hh.

There should be at least 3.7m (12ft) headroom to aid ventilation.

Door openings should be at least 1.2m (4ft) wide so there is plenty of room for a horse to pass through without banging his hips. A stable door should always open outwards so that it can be opened if a horse lies down or gets cast (stuck against the stable wall when he rolls or lies down.) When stabling small ponies, make sure the door is of an appropriate height for them to see over. That sounds obvious, but if a pony is standing with his neck muscles straining, he will become uncomfortable.

A stable should have internal kickboards: preferably full height, as it's amazing how high a horse can kick! Kickboards are used so that if a horse kicks out, he does not put a foot through an external wall.

If a horse habitually kicks out, try and find out what provokes this. Is he worried by his neighbour, or disturbed by something going on outside? You could also think about using special rubber wall mats to minimise the shock of the kick going up his limbs and to limit damage to the stable.

Fresh Air Facts

Look after your and your horse's respiratory systems. You can both be compromised by poor ventilation, dust and spores from bedding and forage and ammonia from urine and droppings. A well-designed stable will increase ventilation without subjecting a horse to draughts.

A stable which provides good ventilation is one which allows frequent changes of air. To create this, the roof should be pitched, not flat, with ventilation outlets at each end of the roof ridge working in conjunction with wall inlets just above the horse's head height.

Stable doors should always have two halves. The top half should not be closed even in bad weather, as this blocks the airflow. Don't shut the top door because you are worried about a horse getting cold: if necessary, put a warmer rug on him.

Bottom doors should have fastenings top and bottom, as some horses can open top fastenings with their teeth. The best system is a sliding bolt at the top and a kick-over latch at the bottom that can be worked without bending down.

Windows should be kept open whenever possible. If practicable, have one at the front and another at the rear. This improves ventilation and gives the occupant another outlook. If necessary, one window can be closed.

Fixtures and Fittings

Internal lighting is essential for many owners. If you don't have an electrical supply a solar-powered system designed for stables could be the answer. It is also possible to have battery-powered lighting. All electrical installations must be horse and rodent-proof, so cables should run through pipes which can't be chewed and switches should be in weatherproof casings, set outside and beyond a horse's reach.

Internal and external tying-up rings are essential. Some yards insist on mucking out and grooming when horses are tied up in their stables. In some cases, this has to be done for safety reasons, but as a matter of routine, it is better for the horse's respiratory system if he is tied up outside so he does not have to breathe in dust, spores and ammonia.

If you feed hay from a net, you need a ring to which it can be tied, set at an appropriate height. If a net is too high, dust and seeds will fall into a horse's eyes whilst he is eating. If it is too low, he may paw at an empty net and become caught.

Automatic watering systems save labour, but unless they include a gauge, you can't tell if your horse is drinking. Water containers range from buckets, either on the ground or wall-mounted, to corner mangers. All feed and water containers must be scrubbed out daily.

Bedding

There is a huge variety of bedding materials available, all with advantages and disadvantages. Don't base your choice purely on purchase price, as there are other factors to consider:

- Horses should be kept in an environment that is as free as possible from dust, mould and spores. You can never eliminate them, but some types of bedding make it easier to keep the stable environment healthy.
- How do you cope with manure disposal? Some types of bedding result in a smaller muck heap than others.
- Do you have ample storage space? Some types of bedding are sold in bulky bales, others in space-saving bags.
- How easy are different types of bedding to manage? Some products generate more wet material for removal than others, resulting in heavier loads and bigger muck heaps.
- Do you have bedding delivered or do you have to collect it? If you collect it, how long is your journey and is the bedding always available?

Material Matters

Horses aren't nesting animals and happily lie down in the field. Even so, some form of bedding must be used to provide warmth and protection from a cold, hard concrete floor.

You can't eliminate dust, but can get a head start through your choice of bedding—though do be aware that some dust-extraction systems are better than others. Buy two or three sample bales before ordering a large load.

Rubber matting makes a good base for any bed. If a horse scrapes through his bedding, matting will help prevent him capping hocks or elbows (scraping them on the concrete when he gets up, which can result in fluid-filled enlargements developing).

There are many different makes, but choose one that is easy to lay and manage. Mats must be lifted at intervals so you can clean out the debris which gathers underneath and disinfect the floor.

Don't use mats without bedding on top unless your vet advises it. They may give enough protection, but some horses are reluctant to stale (urinate) because of the splash factor and rugs will get filthy. Some owners use a smaller amount of bedding than would be used without mats, but whether this works depends on the horse's size and personal habits, the amount of floor space and how often you can remove droppings.

Commonly used bedding materials are:

- **Wheat straw** is relatively cheap and easy to obtain, but must be clean, not dusty. It must be kept dry, or it will develop mould spores. It makes a deep, comfortable bed but isn't as absorbent as some other materials and takes up a lot of storage space.

  Horses will eat wheat straw; a little won't hurt, but it might predispose one who munches all night to colic, as it contains an indigestible woody substance called lignin. Barley straw is less resilient and more palatable so is not a good bedding choice.

- **Chopped, treated straw, flax and hemp products** are easy to handle and are often treated with substances such as eucalyptus to make them unpalatable. They are wrapped in plastic, so stay dry and because they are chopped short, break down quicker than ordinary straw.

- **Wood shavings and wood fibre products** make good beds and are easy to manage. They must be as dust-free as possible. Some take longer to degrade than others.

- **Pellet bedding** can be made from wood or straw. Water must be added to wood pellets so that they break down and fluff up to a much higher volume. Straw pellets are usually used dry and break down as a horse moves around.

- **Chopped cardboard and shredded paper** are dust-free but may not be as absorbent as other types of bedding and may be heavy when wet.

(1) Rubber matting gives a good base for any type of bedding. (2) Wheat straw makes a deep, comfortable bed but is not as absorbent as many other types of bedding material. (3) Hemp bedding is easy to handle and store.

Mucking Out

The right tools can make mucking out much easier. Choose ones which are suitable for the type of bedding; for example, 'basket forks' work well with wood pellets and shavings forks make light work if you don't like donning rubber gloves and picking up piles! Stiff-bristled brooms are useful for sweeping stable floors, but wide, softer-bristled heads may be easier for sweeping a yard.

Choose tools which are substantial enough to do the job but light enough to handle. Make sure handles are the right length for your height and store tools safely so they can't be trodden on by horses or people.

Looking after horses involves a lot of lifting, bending and pushing. Protect your back by dividing large loads into smaller ones and lifting weights correctly:

• Keep feet apart and one leg slightly forward to stay balanced as you lift.
• Don't bend your back whilst lifting.
• Don't twist as you lift.
• Keep your head up—look ahead, not at the load.
• Don't jerk or snatch.
• Don't overload your wheelbarrow. When pushing, drop your shoulders and use your core muscles; don't curve your back.

Methods

There are three mucking out methods: full, semi-litter and deep litter. A full muck-out means all droppings and dirty/wet material is taken out every day. Semi-litter means removing droppings daily but removing wet material once or twice a week. Deep litter means removing droppings and adding fresh bedding on top of old, removing the whole lot at infrequent intervals.

A full muck-out is best, but with the right type of bedding, semi-littering can work. Look at bedding manufacturers' recommendations.

Deep litter is NOT recommended in stables because a build-up of ammonia is harmful to a horse's respiratory system. It may be the only way to manage if a group of horses are kept in a barn and bedded on straw, perhaps during winter. In this case, the barn must be well-ventilated.

Traditionally, beds are made with deep banks at the sides. This is said to help prevent horses getting cast, but opinions vary.

Be careful how you dispose of manure and aim to keep a tidy muck heap.

Muck Heaps

A well-made muck heap takes up less space and rots down more quickly. The classic way is to build a heap in steps, starting at the back and building a layer about 1m wide. Keep it level and when it becomes too high to throw dirty bedding on top, begin another layer in front.

Some yards prefer to park a muck trailer and throw dirty bedding on, emptying the trailer as needed. The type of bedding will affect the amount of discard material; ordinary straw produces most whilst pellet bedding, for example, results in much smaller amounts.

Many yards now have to pay for muck disposal, though some farmers will take well-rotted manure that can be spread straight on the land. Don't try and burn manure, as this contravenes the Clean Air Act 1993. You must also ensure that run-off liquid does not enter water courses.

Fire Risks

Wooden stables, bedding and stored forage are a potential fire hazard. Storage should be organised to minimise the risk of fire spreading: for instance, hay and straw stores should be sited away from other buildings. Every yard should have fire extinguishers at appropriate points. Get advice from your local fire prevention officer on what type to use, how to use them and where to site them, but remember that they are there for emergency action. Always dial 999 or 112 in the event of fire.

4. Feeding

Given the chance, horses would spend most of their time eating. This is not down to greed, but to the way their digestive systems work. They are 'trickle feeders' who need a steady intake of small amounts—which is why grazing or a ready supply of forage to mimic grazing behaviour is so important—rather than eating larger amounts at infrequent intervals.

Remember that horses evolved to live on far less luxurious grazing than we usually provide. Look at environments such as Exmoor!

Your challenge is to provide what your horse needs to help keep him healthy and fit for his job, whether that be equine athlete or companion. Feeding is just one part of the jigsaw and must be looked at alongside an appropriate work/exercise regime, but it is an important part.

Horses are designed to function on a high fibre diet, which is why forage in the form of grass, hay or haylage is so important. You may need to add extra feed and, perhaps, supplements, but clean, good quality forage must always make up most of his diet. Many animals thrive on forage and an appropriate vitamin and mineral supplement alone, but forage should never fall below 75 per cent of the diet even for horses in hard work and rarely needs to fall below 90 per cent.

There may be times when you need to restrict grazing to prevent your horse becoming overweight. Obesity is one of the biggest dangers to horse health, so before you look at what and how much to feed, decide whether your horse is just right, overweight or underweight.

Use a scoring system, known as 'condition scoring' or 'body fat scoring', to decide. You need to feel for fat deposits as well as making

Exmoor ponies living in their natural habitat.

a visual assessment. Horses with caring owners are rarely too thin, but are often overweight. Horses store fat on their neck and topline, over their shoulders, on their ribs, spine, backbone and pelvis area and at the top of the tail.

Follow the guidelines below and if you aren't sure, ask your vet. The best way is to divide your horse into three sections, score each area and divide the total by three to give an average. Do this every fortnight, as when you see a horse every day you don't notice gradual changes.

Use a weigh tape every fortnight, too. Position the tape according to the instructions; it won't be as accurate as a weighbridge, but will tell you whether your horse is maintaining, gaining or losing weight and will also help you work out accurate dosage rates for wormers. Use a weigh tape at the same time each day to get accurate results.

Taking photographs regularly also helps, as it gives a visual record.

Be realistic. A cob is never going to look as slim as a racehorse and you must never starve a horse to try and slim him down.

Winning Scores

Scores can be made from 0–5 (including half marks) or 0–9. Welfare organisations and feed companies provide online advice and videos, but here are guidelines for the 0–5 method.

0   **VERY POOR, EMACIATED.** The rump is sunken, with a deep cavity under the tail. Backbone, ribs and pelvis are prominent and the horse will appear to have a ewe (upside down) neck when this may not be the case.

1   **POOR.** As above, but to a lesser extent.

2   **MODERATE.** The neck is firm but narrow and the rump is flat either side of the spine, though the spine itself is not visible. Ribs may be visible, but not markedly so as in 0 and 1.

3   **GOOD.** The ribs can be felt but are covered, the rump is rounded and the neck is firm, but not cresty.

4   **FAT.** There is a gutter along the back and pelvis and it's very difficult to feel the ribs.

5   **OBESE.** The gutter along the back and pelvis is deep and you can't feel the ribs. There are pads of fat on the crest and/or neck and/or shoulders.

How Much Does He Need?

The rule of thumb is that a horse needs to eat 2–2.5 per cent of his weight in total each day, so a 500kg horse would need 12.5kg daily. As we know, this should comprise mostly forage.

If a horse needs to lose weight, it is better to lower the energy level of his feed (calories) than to go below a 2 per cent daily intake. Grass can sometimes provide more than he needs, especially when you have ideal growing conditions of warmth and rainfall. Researchers now know that restricting grazing time encourages horses to eat faster, so rather than reduce his time in the field, use a grazing muzzle.

Strip grazing can also help. Divide a field into small sections with temporary electric fencing so that each section is thoroughly grazed down before you move the horse to another.

There are so many different types of feed available that deciding what and how much to feed can be confusing. However, think in terms of giving mainly good quality forage together with a constant supply of clean water and you won't go far wrong!

The Golden Rules of Feeding

1. Always feed plenty of good quality forage.
2. Always make sure the horse has a supply of clean, fresh water.
3. Maintain your horse's weight so that he is in correct condition.
4. If you give hard feed, offer small meals at regular intervals – don't

Strip grazing can help if you are trying to reduce a horse's weight.

divide it into large meals. Don't feed more than 2kg hard feed in one meal or you will overload the horse's digestive system.

Haylage is baled before the drying completes and wrapped in plastic to exclude air.

5. Any changes to the diet should be made gradually, mixing a small quantity of the new hay or feed with the old and gradually altering the proportions.

6. Feed according to condition, size, type, work and age: for instance, horses up to three years of age, breeding animals and old horses have different nutritional requirements, so get advice.

7. Increase exercise before you increase feed, not the other way round.

8. You can feed to complement or make the most of a horse's temperament, but you can't change it. Get advice from a qualified nutritionist.

9. Horses appreciate routine, so try and feed at the same time each day. Good DIY yard owners may ask you to feed at a certain time or prepare and leave feeds so this can be done.

10. If your horse is on box rest, feed according to your vet's advice.

Forage and Fibre

Both hay and haylage are made from cut, baled grass. The difference is that hay is dried before baling whilst haylage is baled before the drying completes and wrapped in plastic or sealed in a plastic bag to exclude air.

Hay has the advantage of a higher fibre content, but must be stored in dry conditions and will never be totally dust-free. Nutritionists advise that it should be soaked or steamed to overcome this. Even spray hosing your haynet for five minutes can help to reduce some dust, but this will not be enough to protect a horse with any level of respiratory problem.

If you want to retain the nutritional value, soak hay for a short time— up to an hour. If you want to reduce the feed value, perhaps because your horse needs to lose weight, soak it for 12 hours. Soak every batch in clean water.

The feed value of dry hay depends on the grass value, its maturity at cutting and how well it is made. Some owners, particularly those of competition animals, have hay supplies analysed so they know exactly what it supplies.

In theory, steamed or soaked oat straw makes a good forage for good doers and those who need to lose weight. In practice, it is very hard to find.

Haylage has a high water content and so weight for weight, is lower in fibre than hay. It doesn't need soaking or steaming and should have a guaranteed nutritional level, whereas hay loses some of this as it ages.

Always discard haylage which shows signs of mould or which smells bad. This is usually caused by the wrapping being pierced so that air is allowed in. A good supplier will exchange bad bales for new ones.

Silage, fed mainly to dairy cattle, should not be fed to horses. Manufacturing methods mean there is a risk of it containing micro-organisms that cause botulism—something which does not affect cattle but may be fatal to horses.

If possible, feed hay or haylage from the ground. This mimics his grazing action, which produces a better pattern of wear on his teeth and helps minimise tension in his neck muscles. Using a special hay feeding station can help minimise waste.

However, feeding from ground level isn't always practical and you may need to use a haynet. Tie it as shown, so it stays safe and secure, and check that the height is correct for your horse. He should not have to raise his head high to eat, as this increases the risk that seeds will fall in his ears and eyes and also puts strain on his neck muscles. Nor should it be too low; an empty haynet hangs lower than a full one and you do not want to risk him pawing at it and getting caught up.

How to tie a haynet securely. Tie the haynet directly to the ring, but tie your pony to a piece of string attached to the ring.

If you want to slow down his eating rate, use a specially designed small mesh net. These are sometimes called haylage nets. Alternatively, fill an ordinary haynet and place it inside another for the same effect.

Sugar beet must be soaked according to the feed manufacturer's instructions.

Forage is important because it is high in fibre. There are also high fibre, bagged forage feeds available, marketed under different names. They range from chaff made from chopped hay mixed with chopped oat straw to dried, chopped grass. Alfalfa (lucerne) has a high feed value; when mixed with chopped hay and straw it increases the nutritional value of a forage feed. It can also be fed alone, chopped or in pellet form, when appropriate.

Soaked sugar beet, preferably unmolassed, is another good source of fibre. It must be soaked according to the manufacturer's instructions. In most cases, pellets should be soaked for 24 hours and shreds for 12 hours.

You will also find 'quick soak' sugar beet which is ready to use after a much shorter period. All soaked sugar beet should be fed within 24 hours, especially in hot weather, or it may ferment. ***Do not ignore soaking-time instructions: dry sugar beet swells when water is added. It is still palatable when dry and will swell in your horse's stomach, which will often lead to colic***

Water

It's vital that your horse ***always*** has access to clean, fresh water. Change the supply at least daily, even if it looks clean. A 500kg horse needs about 20 litres water daily, though may drink more. If his diet has a high moisture content, he may drink less, but should still have constant access to water. Dehydration is dangerous—*see* Chapter 5.

Extra Feed

Horses in hard work and those who don't maintain a correct weight on forage alone may need extra feed, often called hard feed. Cobs and native ponies usually maintain weight much more easily than Thoroughbredtypes, but if your horse loses weight when you don't want him to, or you can't maintain his weight, check that he is in good health as well as checking his diet. This may mean calling in your vet.

In particular, it is important to check that his mouth and teeth are in good condition and that he doesn't carry a heavy parasite burden (*see* Chapter 5).

The easiest way to supply extra fuel is in the form of compound feed. This can be formulated into coarse mix, which looks like equine muesli, or as cubes, sometimes called nuts. Mixes are usually more expensive than cubes and most animals will eat either, though fussy eaters may find mixes more tempting.

Before compound feed was invented, owners fed oats or barley usually mixed with chaff. These are referred to as straight cereals or, simply, straights. The advantage of compound feed is that it is designed to supply everything your horse needs when fed at the manufacturer's recommended amount for his weight. The nutritional value of a make and type of feed remains constant, but the value of straight cereals will vary between batches.

In the Bag

Information about compound feed will be on the back of the bag. There is a statutory statement which includes things such as the name of the feed, indicating the type of animal it is meant for; whether it is a complete feed or—as in most cases—designed to be fed as a sole concentrate source alongside forage; the name and address of the manufacturer; bag weight, best before date and date of manufacture.

Compound feed may be in the form of mix (left) or cubes.

You will also find details of the feed's nutrient analysis. By law, manufacturers only have to declare crude protein, crude fibre, oil, ash, copper and vitamins A, D and E, though some give more information. Don't be confused by the reference to ash: you won't find any in the feed! It refers to the mineral value, determined by burning the feed to leave a mineral residue.

Added Extras

If you feed less than the recommended weight of compound feed or your horse lives and works happily on a forage diet, he will lack some vitamins and minerals. The easiest way to supply these is by feeding a broad spectrum vitamin and mineral supplement or a feed balancer.

A balancer is a concentrated form of compound feed fed in very small quantities, so it meets your horse's needs but adds far fewer calories. Get expert advice on which will best suit your horse.

Supplements

There are so many supplements available, from products designed to 'promote calmness' to those said to support hoof or joint problems, that many owners are understandably confused. They are officially called complementary feeding stuffs, but the colloquial term supplements is generally used and accepted.

There is no such thing as a miracle product and the only extra every horse needs is salt. Some will be present in compound feed, but not enough to meet requirements. General advice is to provide 25g daily in feed or free access to a salt lick. Horses in hard work may need electrolytes to replace salts lost through sweat.

Calmers are the most controversial supplement. Get expert advice before using one and check first that any problem is not down to your management or riding. For instance, is your horse turned out enough to let off excess energy? If he is sensitive and/or forward going, are you experienced and competent enough to ride him or do you need help from a good instructor to hopefully improve your technique and confidence?

If you compete, be careful that a supplement does not contravene competition rules on forbidden substances. If in doubt, ask your vet.

5.
Health
Matters

Looking after your horse's health is a combination of good management, preventive health care and knowing when to seek professional advice. All owners need a support team, headed by an equine vet. You'll need other professionals— in particular, a registered farrier, who may well work with your vet in cases of lameness—but your vet must always be the first person you call on if you are worried.

It's easy to find information about health care and problems via the internet, but be careful. There is also a lot of misinformation! It's great to discuss issues, but legally, only a vet can give a diagnosis and perform surgical treatment. There are professionals who can treat a horse under veterinary approval; for instance, your vet may recommend that a horse needs physiotherapy and will recommend a suitably qualified person.

The Right Kit

You should have two first aid kits at your yard, one for your horse and one for people. They should be clearly distinguished. Ideally, you should also have a separate equine first aid kit for travelling which can live in your horsebox or towing vehicle.

You may want to ask your vet what you should include in your horse's first aid kit. The following is a good selection of items, but remember to replace anything that is used.

- *A card* on which you have written your vet's contact numbers. These should be programmed into your mobile phone, along with your own In Case of Emergency (ICE) numbers—but doubling up means more than one person has access to them.
- *Digital thermometer.*
- *Antiseptic,* as recommended by your vet. Antiseptic wipes are especially useful for a travelling first aid kit.
- *Water-soluble wound gel*, as recommended by your vet.
- Large roll of *cotton wool.*
- *Scissors* with curved ends.
- *Gamgee* or similar.
- *Poultice.*
- *Duct tape* for securing poultice.
- *Dressings*—non-stick dressings to cover wounds; self-adhesive bandages; cool bandages or packs with a cooling action to apply to limbs; cotton stretch bandages.

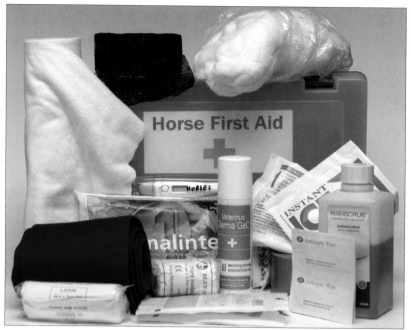
Always replace any used items in your first aid kit.

Signs of Health

To recognise when your horse is ill or injured, you need to know the signs of a healthy horse. Things to look for are:

- Temperature, pulse and respiration (TPR) should be within the following ranges for an adult horse at rest:
  Temperature 37–38°C / **Pulse** 24–42 / **Respiration** 8–16
  Breaths should be smooth and relaxed.
- He should be alert and interested in what's going on. A horse who is relaxed or dozing will look interested when something attracts his attention, but one who is ill will often remain uninterested and lethargic.
- His appetite should be normal.
- His coat should be normal for him and for the season. Don't worry if a healthy pony grows a thick winter coat, but if a sleek coat suddenly becomes dull and stands away from the skin when there is no change in the weather, check his other signs.
- His eyes should be clear and bright with no discharge.
- Mucous membranes—the gums, and round the eyes—should be salmon pink and if pressure is applied to the gums and then released, colour should return within a couple of seconds.

- He should pass droppings regularly and they should be of reasonable consistency. As a guideline, they should break when they hit the floor, not be liquid or in hard balls—though a flush of grass will often change the consistency. He should also be urinating normally, without straining. Urine should be its normal colour, which can range from pale to brownish yellow. If this suddenly changes, especially if you suspect the presence of blood, call your vet for advice.
- He should be in good condition, neither overweight nor underweight, as explained in Chapter 4.
- He should not be dehydrated. The pinch test is useful: pinch and release a fold of skin at the base of the neck. It should spring back into shape immediately. If it doesn't, your horse is badly dehydrated. However, this only picks up an extreme case: even a two per cent level of dehydration will affect a horse's performance, which underlines the importance of allowing permanent access to fresh water.

Checking Figures

Take your horse's TPR at rest regularly so that you know what's normal for him within the parameters above. You should always stand in a safe position when handling a horse and whenever possible, get someone to stand at his head. Children should not try and cope alone.

To take a horse's temperature, grease a digital thermometer with petroleum jelly. Approach your horse from the side and run your hand along his hindquarters—don't insert the thermometer without warning!

Still standing to the side, move his tail over and take the thermometer in your other hand. Insert it gently, holding it at a slight angle for security. When you hear the sound indicating the reading is complete, remove the thermometer gently.

To take a pulse, feel for the facial artery which passes under the jaw and press against it with the flat of your first three fingers. Take a reading for one minute or, if this is impossible, count the pulse rate for 15 seconds and multiply by four.

If you suspect your horse has laminitis, feel and measure the digital pulse as shown above. This can be hard to find, so ask your farrier or vet to show you how.

To measure respiration, stand behind and to one side of your horse and count each rise and fall of the flank as one breath.

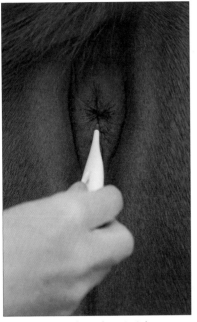

It's important to learn how to take your horse's temperature.

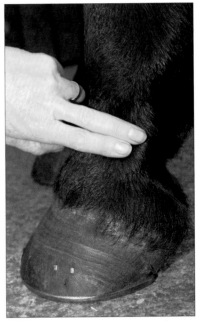

Ask your vet or farrier to show you how to take a horse's digital pulse.

Preventive Measures

It's essential to protect your horse through vaccination, good farriery, dental care and a correct worming programme, whatever his age or job.

Vaccination

The British Equine Veterinary Association says it is important to protect against tetanus, equine influenza and, ideally, equine herpes virus. Tetanus, caused by bacteria invading the system through cuts and puncture wounds, can be fatal and you as well as your horse should be vaccinated!

Equine flu is a contagious viral respiratory disease that affects a horse's respiratory system. Apart from being an essential safeguard, vaccination is mandatory under the rules of many disciplines and competition rules.

Equine herpes virus is also a viral respiratory disease. Some types of this virus can cause abortion and paralysis.

In some circumstances, your vet may recommend other vaccinations.

Farriery

Regular hoof care is a vital part of keeping your horse sound, whether or not he is shod. Your job is to pick out and inspect your horse's feet every day—including before and after you ride—so you can spot problems which need a farrier's or vet's attention.

Some people believe all horses should be able to work unshod, but it should come down to the individual horse, the characteristics of his feet and his workload. Your farrier is the best person to tell you what would suit your horse. Legally, only a registered farrier can shoe a horse. It is recommended that you *always* use a registered farrier, including for trims on unshod animals.

Your farrier should see your horse every four to six weeks and trim/ shoe him according to his needs. It is not just a case of preventing cracks, but of maintaining the correct foot balance to keep him sound.

A balanced foot is one which enables the best weight distribution. To achieve it, your farrier will look at the horse's conformation and movement, as well as the shape of his foot, to take into account the angles of his limbs. In some cases of unsoundness, remedial shoeing to give extra support and improve balance may be carried out. Your

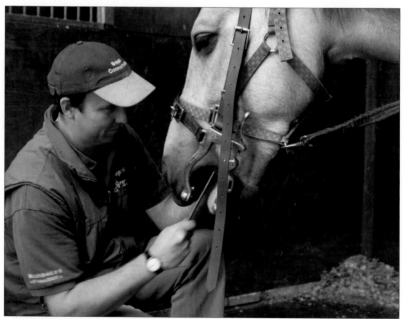

Routine dental checks are an important part of preventive health care, but if you think your horse has a problem, get him checked immediately.

vet will usually take X-rays and the type of remedial shoeing will be decided on after discussion between your vet and farrier.

It takes an expert eye to tell the difference between feet that need a farrier's attention and bad conformation. One of the commonest problems, which can fall into either or both categories, is the horse with long toes and collapsed heels. This puts pressure on the back of the foot.

A farrier needs a dry, level, well-lit area in which to work. You can't expect a farrier to do a perfect job if asked to trim or shoe a horse in a field.

Many riders use studs for fast work, competing and jumping to give horses extra grip. Ask your farrier's advice about which type to use, as it is important to get the right balance between giving a horse security and preventing his limbs from being jarred. As a general guideline, pointed studs are used on harder ground and square studs when the going is soft. Studs can't compensate for unsafe going.

If you need to remove a loose shoe to minimise the risk of injury, ask an experienced person to do it for you. Where appropriate, your farrier will show you how it is done and the tools that are needed.

Dental Care

Unlike ours, horses' teeth grow throughout their lives. Although grazing causes wear, it isn't enough—nature needs a hand. A horse's lower jaw is narrower than his upper one, so when he grazes, the outside edges of the upper cheek teeth and the inside edges of the lower ones may be worn in a pattern with sharp edges/hooks. This can cause rubs and lacerations and because the horse can't chew properly, he will be susceptible to digestive problems and colic. To prevent these problems, your horse must be checked by an equine vet or a BEVA-qualified equine dental technician (EDT) so that sharp edges can be rasped smooth and any other necessary measures taken.

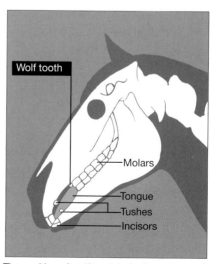

The position of wolf teeth in the horse's mouth.

Many horses have wolf teeth, which are small, vestigial premolars. They can cause problems if they interfere with the bit, but are usually easy to remove. Opinions vary on whether they should be removed as a preventive measure, so discuss this with your vet. Some procedures require a horse to be sedated and only a vet can do this.

BEVA recommends that routine dental care should be started in a horse's first year, followed by annual or six-monthly check-ups according to the individual's needs. Your vet or EDT will advise you, but if you think your horse has a problem between scheduled visits, get immediate advice: don't wait for your next appointment.

Warning signs of discomfort or pain include tilting the head, resistance and dropping food out of the mouth (quidding). There may be other reasons other than a dental problem, but it is always best to check.

Worming

You can never eliminate parasites, but you do need to control the worm burden. We now know that in most cases, the best way to do this is by a combination of removing droppings from fields, targeted worming and faecal worm egg counts (FWECs). The latest research points to the following as good practice:

- Don't overstock fields.
- Remove droppings regularly—preferably daily but at least weekly.
- Rotate grazing with sheep or cattle if possible to interrupt parasites' life cycle.
- All equines should be wormed in late autumn against encysted redworm, as FWECs don't detect these.
- All equines should be wormed annually against tapeworm, preferably in the late autumn/winter.
- Always worm according to your horse's weight. The most accurate way to assess weight is by using a weighbridge; equine clinics and larger practices will have them on site and most allow clients to use them without charging. If that's not possible, use a weigh tape and position it according to the manufacturer's instructions.
- Don't overdose or underdose. Both will increase the likelihood of resistance to wormers, overdosing can result in diarrhoea or colic and underdosing will be ineffective.

Get your vet's advice on the best worming regime for your horse.

• Don't assume that all classes of wormers treat all types of worms. They don't—get advice from your vet.

Not all wormers are safe or suitable for youngstock. Again, get advice from your vet. Advice is also needed if your horse is kept on a livery yard where owners are responsible for their own animals' worming programmes or if you run a yard with a constantly changing equine population.

Worming will only be effective if you ensure your horse takes in the correct amount—if he spits half of it out, you've underdosed. Palatable wormers and those in tablet form are easier to administer.

Dispose of empty packaging carefully, as horse wormers can be poisonous to other species.

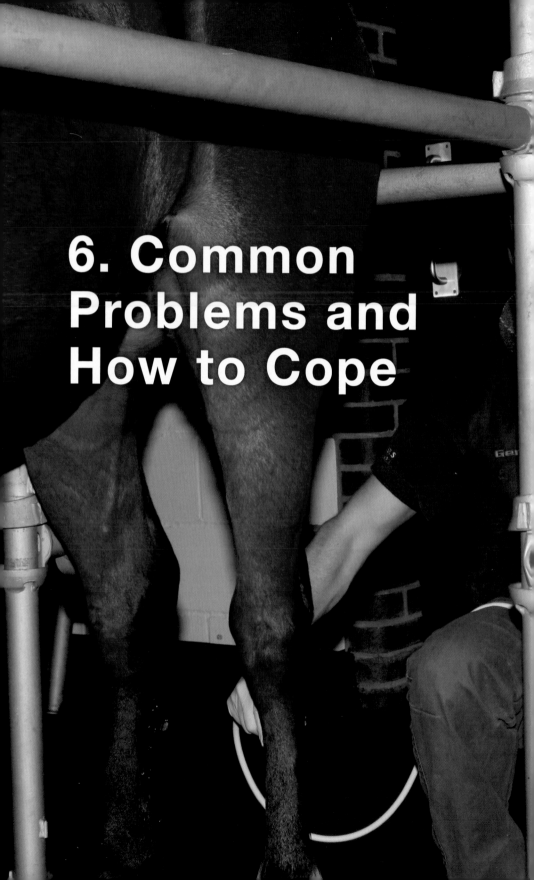

6. Common Problems and How to Cope

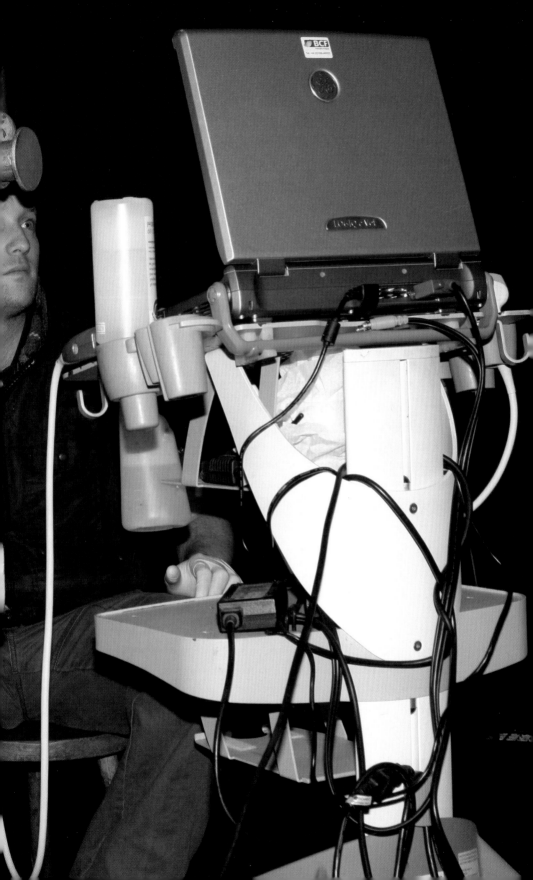

It's worrying when a horse is ill or injured, but try and keep calm so you can do the best for him. Minor injuries can often be dealt with at home, but if you are not sure whether an injury or condition is serious or are not sure how to deal with it, call your vet.

Any vet will tell you that it is better to ask for advice than to risk an injury being worse than you thought, or illness becoming worse. For instance, a puncture wound caused by penetration of a sharp object may look insignificant, but it could be deep. If left, deep-seated infection may develop. Early diagnosis and treatment gives your horse a head start to recovery, so if in doubt, call!

The more information your vet has, the easier it is to give advice over the phone. This is where mobile phones can be useful—for instance, if you are at a show and your horse cuts himself, your vet may ask you to take and send a picture of a wound. This will help the vet decide whether you can carry out first aid and take the horse home or to a veterinary clinic for attention, or must have an on-site visit.

If your horse seems off-colour, or you think he may have colic, it will help your vet's over-the-phone assessment if you can take the animal's temperature before calling. Only attempt this if you can do it safely.

This chapter can provide only a short overview of conditions a horse owner may have to deal with. Even so, it can make alarming reading— but it's better to be aware of what could happen than to be caught out because you didn't spot a possible problem.

It's an Emergency!

Let's look at the worst scenarios first. There are some situations which *always* require veterinary attention.

Colic

This describes any sort of abdominal pain and can range from mild discomfort to a life-threatening episode requiring surgery. Signs may include any or several of the following:

- Raised temperature.
- Sweating.
- Stamping and shifting weight.
- Looking at, biting or cow-kicking the flanks.
- Rolling whilst showing signs of discomfort.

- Standing as if trying to urinate.
- Failing to pass droppings.

Action—Take the horse's temperature if safe to do so. Call your vet and act on instructions until he or she arrives.

Severe Wounds

—which means:

- Any which is causing severe lameness.
- A wound which is more than 5cm (2in) long and has gone through the skin.
- Presence or suspected presence of a foreign body, perhaps a piece of wood or a nail.
- A wound in or near a joint.
- Heavy bleeding.
- Bleeding in spurts, which is a sign of arterial blood loss.
- Any wound in a horse who is not protected against tetanus.

Action—If blood is spurting and you or someone else knows how to apply a pressure bandage, do so. If not, apply pressure with a clean pad, if one is available, until your vet arrives.

If a nail or other foreign body causes a penetration wound, it's best to leave it until you've spoken to your vet; sometimes, trying to remove it can cause more problems. The exception is when a nail penetrates the foot and the horse is weight-bearing, because it may be pushed farther in. Be careful not to break off the nail and when you've removed it, mark the entrance point.

Bleeding from the nose not associated with fast exercise may mean that the horse has suffered a blow to the head, such as a kick from a field mate. Call your vet immediately.

Copious bleeding after fast work is usually due to exercise-induced pulmonary haemorrhage. Again, you need veterinary advice.

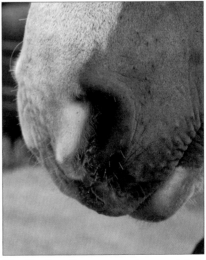

Bleeding from the nose may be associated with a blow to the head.

Suspected Fracture / Severe Lameness

If a horse can't bear weight on one limb or suddenly goes badly lame, keep him still. Unless the limb appears deformed/is held at a strange angle, check that there are no stones or other foreign bodies lodged in the foot.

Lameness usually shows only in trot so any lameness in walk should be treated as severe and dealt with as above. Try to keep calm, as severe lameness can be caused by things other than severe injury, such as an abscess in the foot.

Action—If there is no simple cause, such as a stone which can be removed, call your vet. Don't try and walk the horse to a yard until your vet gets there. If you are on a public road—where, hopefully, you will be wearing high-vis clothing—keep to the side of the road. Call the police so they know where you are and can, if necessary, send someone to help keep you and other road users safe until the vet arrives.

Collapse or Unable to Get Up

Action—Call your vet immediately. If you are on a road, also call the police, as above.

Choke

This self-explanatory term means a horse seems to have a blockage in his oesophagus: if it happened to you, you would say your food had 'gone down the wrong way.' Signs include stopping eating when part of the way through a feed, stretching the neck and looking uncomfortable and food and saliva appearing from the nostrils.

Action— Remove any food if stabled and call your vet. Fortunately, most cases clear themselves fairly quickly, but don't take chances. Your vet may suggest you watch the horse for a short time and call back if things don't improve—unless, of course, the horse is in distress—but making the call will alert your vet.

Equine Rhabdomyolysis Syndrome

The colloquial names for this sudden-onset condition are azoturia or set-fast. It is similar to muscle cramp in the hindquarters area and can be so painful that the horse refuses to move and shows other signs of pain, such as sweating. In some cases, it can be difficult to distinguish ERS from colic, but in either case—call your vet.

Action—If you suspect your horse has suffered an attack of ERS and are at or near home, place a rug or your jacket, if available, over his quarters. If it is a mild attack and he is stiff but able and reasonably willing to move, lead him into his stable and keep his back and hindquarters warm with a rug.

If he can't move, keep him warm and call your vet for further instructions. Never ignore even a mild attack, as your vet will want to take blood samples straight away.

Laminitis

This condition is very painful and must be treated by your vet at the first signs. In simple terms, it is inflammation of the laminae inside the foot. It is often linked to obesity, but it can be linked to other causes, including concussion, Cushing's syndrome and problems associated with foaling.

Signs range from lameness and a raised digital pulse to, in severe cases, the horse refusing to move and taking a backward-leaning stance to relieve pressure on his feet. Treatment includes medication and in some cases, remedial farriery.

Action—Call your vet immediately.

Preventive Action—Monitor your horse's weight and maintain an appropriate exercise regime.

Grass Sickness

This potentially fatal condition is thought to be caused by a soil-borne bacteria. It produces symptoms similar to colic and in acute cases, the horse will lose weight drastically and quickly.

Action—Call your vet immediately so that the correct diagnosis can be made.

Preventive Action—Grass sickness can affect any equine, but most commonly strikes those aged between five and nine years. The danger period for its occurrence is roughly May to July, though it is also seen at other times.

Your vet may advise moving animals kept where grass sickness cases have occurred to different premises during high-risk times, if possible. You may also be advised to feed hay or haylage as well as allowing the horse to graze.

Other Common Problems

This section gives you information about problems you may have to deal with. Not all will be serious, but remember that anything has the potential to become so. Once again: *if in doubt, call your vet.*

Wounds

For non-emergency wounds, follow the four Cs: <u>C</u>lot, <u>C</u>heck, <u>C</u>lean and <u>C</u>over.

1. Stop immediate bleeding.
2. Check the wound's position and size and try and assess if it might need stitching or stapling.
3. Wash gently with suitable antiseptic solution or, if antiseptic is not available, boiled, cooled water to which salt has been added—one teaspoon of salt to 500ml (just under one pint) water. Allow water to fall from above the wound to clean out dirt which may cause infection. *Don't* use water at high pressure, as this may send dirt deeper into the wound.
4. If you are calling your vet, apply a clean pad and bandage to keep the area clean unless you are applying pressure to restrict arterial bleeding. *Don't* apply powders or creams, as your vet will have to clean them off to inspect the wound.
5. Wounds which do not need closing often heal best if a water-soluble wound gel is applied. These are marketed under various names.

There may be times when a vet thinks a visit may be necessary and it turns out to be a minor problem. You can't expect your vet to be psychic and in any case, should never begrudge a call-out fee. It's far better to be safe than sorry.

Lameness

This is the most common reason for horses being off work. Whilst it isn't always an emergency and some cases may resolve quickly when a horse is rested, it's always best to ask your vet's advice. This enables a vet to put together a picture of what might be happening.

If you aren't sure which is the affected leg, watch the horse being trotted away and then back to you on a loose lead rope. A horse who is lame in a foreleg will lift his head as the lame leg meets the ground and lower it as the sound leg hits the ground. An easy way to remember this is that his head '<u>s</u>inks on the <u>s</u>ound leg.'

It's more difficult to spot when a horse is lame in both front legs, but he will have a shorter stride than usual and be reluctant to go forward.

Hindleg lameness is the most difficult to identify and you need to see the horse trotted away from you. He will raise the hip on the lame side more obviously, to try and avoid taking much weight on that leg.

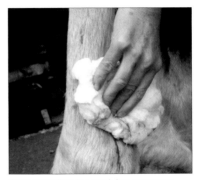

Stop bleeding by applying pressure, using a clean pad if possible.

The most common site of lameness is in the foot, perhaps due to an abscess or laminitis. In this case, there is likely to be a stronger-than-normal digital pulse.

A vet may use flexion tests—where a limb is held and flexed for a short time before the horse is trotted away—to help identify the site of the lameness.

Cushing's Disease

Commonly affects animals over 15 years old, this endocrine system disorder is more common in ponies than in horses. Signs may include puzzling bouts of laminitis that can't be linked to the usual causes; lethargy; and increased drinking and urination. The horse's coat often becomes longer and may also become curly.

Your vet will test for the disease and may suggest medication. Management is important and you may need to clip all year round to keep him comfortable. It is important to do all you can to support the immune system because of the effects Cushing's has on it. Again, your vet will help.

Sweet Itch

This common condition is an allergic reaction to the biting midge Culicoides, which is active during

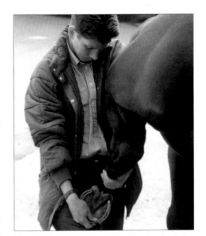

Your vet may carry out a flexion test to help identify the seat of lameness.

mild weather. It causes itching and in severe cases, a sufferer will rub until affected areas—usually the mane and tail—are raw and bleeding. Preventive measures may be enough to control mild cases, but if you can't keep your horse comfortable this way, talk to your vet. Medication can be prescribed and researchers are getting close to finding a vaccination against sweet itch.

Preventive measures include:

- If your horse is stabled part of the time, keep him in at dawn and dusk, when the midges are most active.
- If possible, avoid grazing near water, as midges love it. If this is impossible, follow other guidance scrupulously.
- Use a long-lasting fly repellent and ask your vet for recommendations.
- Use a stretch body cover and, if necessary, a hood designed from special fabric which midges can't bite through. Ordinary fly rugs are not enough.

Rain Scald, Mud Fever and Cracked Heels

These skin conditions are caused by bacteria called Dermatophilus congolensis and show as a sticky secretion causing tufts of hair and/or scabs. Your vet may want to take a skin sample to confirm a diagnosis. The usual treatment is to clip affected areas, wash with anti-bacterial scrub to remove scabs and keep the area dry. In severe cases, antibiotics may be needed.

Leg wraps which wick moisture away and help the area dry more quickly can be useful in managing mud fever.

Ringworm

Although it isn't serious in itself, ringworm is a nuisance. Contrary to the name, no parasites are involved: it is a highly infectious fungal

A special sweet itch rug or stretch cover will help prevent midges biting your horse.

Ringworm is a fungal infection that can be spread from horses to humans.

condition that can be spread between species. If your horse gets ringworm, you could too!

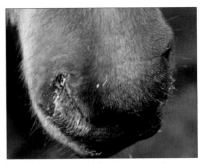

Never ignore nasal discharge, as it may be a sign of a major problem, such as strangles.

The first signs that a horse has ringworm are usually raised tufts of hair, often in areas where tack touches. When the hair falls out, the skin underneath is scaly or bald. Your vet will probably want to take a sample to confirm a diagnosis and treatment ranges from medicated washes to medication.

Everything that the horse has been in contact with must be cleaned with a solution that kills ringworm. This includes tack, rugs and grooming brushes.

Ensuring that every horse has his own tack, grooming kit and clothing helps prevent the spread of ringworm.

Sarcoids

These unsightly growths must never be ignored. Always get your vet to look at a suspected sarcoid, as there are different options for treatment. Never try and treat them yourself.

Strangles

This infectious disease can prove fatal. Signs include a high temperature, nasal discharge and abscesses in the head and neck area. Always call your vet if you suspect strangles.

The End of the Road

At some time in your horse-owning life, you may have to make the last decision you can for your horse. Euthanasia is never easy to come to terms with, whether it is a forced decision due to injury or untreatable illness, or one you have to make because your horse no longer has a quality of life. If you are at or near home, your own vet will help you make the right decision and guide you through all that needs to be done. If you are away from home—perhaps at a competition—and have to rely on an emergency vet, remember that he or she will have the experience and knowledge to help you do the best for your horse.

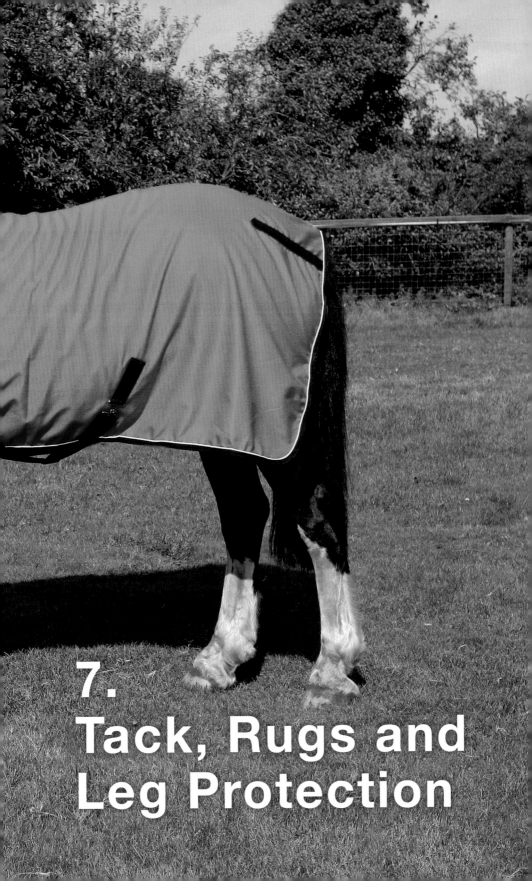

7.
Tack, Rugs and Leg Protection

Choosing, fitting and caring for tack and other equipment is an important part of caring for your horse. Everything you use needs to be suitable for the purpose, fit correctly and be in good condition. Tick these boxes and you will help keep your horse sound and comfortable—which also means he will work well and happily.

Fit for the Job

Whilst tack-fitting is not a medical issue, it is part of good management and preventive health care. In particular, a badly-fitting saddle can cause problems ranging from muscle damage to lameness. If a horse is uncomfortable, he will adjust his stance to try and compensate, which may put extra stress on a particular part of the body or limb.

Bits and bridles may also cause problems if they are the wrong size or wrongly adjusted. For instance, a bit which is too small will pinch his lips and press the inside of his cheeks against his teeth. A browband which is too short will pinch his ears and cause resistance. Small, constant niggles of discomfort can have a much bigger knock-on effect.

Saddles

Your saddle must fit both your horse and you and be suitable for a purpose, whether that be general purpose (GP), dressage or jumping. The best way to ensure its fit and suitability is to get the advice of a knowledgeable saddle-fitter, ideally one who holds the Society of Master Saddlers fitting qualification.

A saddle's fit changes according to whether a horse gains or loses weight and muscle tone, so you need to recognise a saddle which fits well—and indications that there may be a problem—so that you can tell when you need advice on whether it needs adjusting. Fit should be assessed when the horse is moving as well as when he is standing, so you need an observant helper to watch you ride—and, of course, you can ask someone to film you.

Here are some things to keep in mind:
- Most saddles are built on a frame, called a tree. This must be the correct width. If it is too narrow, it will pinch and if it is too wide, it will come down too low on his back. If a horse has muscle wastage on his back he will need a fitting strategy which allows the muscle

to develop again, so get expert advice. Using a narrower (tighter) saddle would only make the problem worse.

- The tree must also have the correct profile so that it follows the shape of your horse's back. If he has a flat back, he needs a saddle with a flat profile and if his back is more curved, the tree must be too. A saddler can often make adjustments to the flocking, but it can't compensate for an unsuitable tree.

- A saddle must not restrict the horse's movement when you ride and should be designed to spread your weight over as wide an area as possible.

Your saddle should fit your horse, suit your proportions and be balanced correctly.

- The lowest part of the seat should be in the centre of the saddle, so you are not tipped backwards or forward. A saddler will be able to make adjustments to balance a saddle if everything else is correct.

- A saddle should sit evenly, not over to one side. Sometimes, it takes an expert eye to tell whether slipping is caused by saddle imbalance, lameness in the horse or a rider putting more weight on one stirrup than the other. Research has shown that saddle slip is often related to hindlimb lameness.

- The gullet should clear the full length of the horse's spine and there should be sufficient clearance at both the pommel and the cantle.

- There are many designs of treeless and semi-treed saddles. Some seem to work well but some cause problems. You can't assume that a treeless saddle will fit or suit every horse and rider, and *every* saddle must be balanced correctly.

- The type of girth, girthing arrangement and design of numnah or pad used can affect saddle fit. Again, get advice from an expert fitter.

Bits and Bridles

You'll find in-depth information about bits and bridles in *The Pony Club Guide to Bits & Bitting* but here are some pointers to help keep your horse comfortable and avoid the risk of irritation and injury:

- Bits must be well-made and in good condition.

- Whatever type of bit you use, it must be the right size—long enough to prevent the horse's lips being pinched, but not so long that it slides from side to side in the mouth.
- The bit must also be adjusted at the correct height. Adjust it so it fits snugly into the corners of the mouth, then check that the mouthpiece lies comfortably across the bars of the mouth and tongue without coming into contact with canine teeth (tushes). Canine teeth are found in geldings, but a few mares have them, too.
- If the mouthpiece has a single joint, this should rest on the centre of the tongue. The same applies to the lozenge or link of a double-jointed mouthpiece. If the bit is too wide, this won't happen.
- Bridles are sold in standard sizes, but to get a perfect fit, you may need to mix and match parts. For instance, a pony with a broad forehead and small muzzle may need a pony or cob-size headpiece but a full-size browband. When a bridle is correctly adjusted:
  - The browband should be long enough to prevent the ears being pinched.
  - There should be four fingers' width between the throatlatch (pronounced throat*lash*) and the horse's face.
  - There should be at least a finger's width between the top of a cavesson or Flash noseband and the bottom of the facial bones. A noseband should not be so tight it clamps the jaws shut and prevents the horse flexing his jaw.

(1) A well-fitting bridle which does not pinch sensitive areas will ensure your horse's comfort. (2) You should be able to fit a hand's width between the throatlatch and your horse's face.

Leg Protection

You need to protect a horse's legs from injury with boots or bandages:

- *When travelling.* The exceptions are mares with foals at foot; unshod youngstock and any other unshod, unhandled horse; horses travelled very long distances by professional transporters in vehicles designed for this purpose. If in doubt, get advice.
- *If a horse is young and/or unbalanced or doesn't move straight.* An inexperienced or unbalanced horse is more likely to strike into himself, as is a horse who moves badly.
- *When jumping or doing fast work*, as the risk of injury is obviously greater.
- *When lungeing*, as he is working on a relatively small, continuous circle. Also, you usually have less control at the end of a lunge rein then when you are riding and a horse may have a buck to let off steam when you start, especially if he is fresh.
- *Some owners put boots on horses before turning them out*, but there is a risk that if dirt gets trapped between the boot and the leg for long periods, it can cause rubs and skin infections. Boots worn for long periods can also cause overheating. Weigh up the pros and cons; if a horse can only be turned out for short periods and is likely to explode, boots could be a good precaution. However, there is a fine line between protection and the sort of over-protection which may end up causing more problems.
- *All boots must be the correct size* for your horse's leg conformation.

Bandages or Boots?

Boots are usually quick and easy to apply, but there are times when correctly applied bandages may be better—so practise your skills. In general, boots give protection and bandages give protection and some support. If leg bandages are put on too tightly, they can cause injury. Boots which are too tight or too loose can also cause problems, but are usually easier to adjust.

Although it may sound obvious, check that you put on boots the right way round! The general rule is that straps on front boots should be fastened so that the ends point towards the hindlegs and straps on hind boots should be secured so the ends point away from the front legs. This is because boots are designed to conform to the shape of the limbs; also, fastening them this way means they are less likely to pull undone.

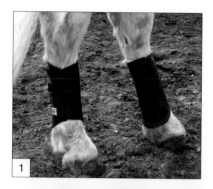

(1) Brushing boots should have reinforced strike pads over the cannon bone area.
(2) Fetlock boots are designed to protect the fetlock joints only. (3) Overreach boots can offer protection, but some trainers feel they should not be used when going cross-country. (4) Tendon boots protect this vulnerable area.

The five main categories of boots are:

- **Brushing boots** are, as the name suggests, designed to protect horses who brush (strike one leg against its partner because of conformation, weakness or both.) They should have a reinforced strike pad in the area which covers the inside of the cannon bone.

- **Fetlock boots** are a shortened version covering just the fetlock area. Some riders use them in preference to brushing boots because they want to protect the fetlock joint, but believe a horse will be more careful if he hits a pole with the unprotected area of his leg. This is not an acceptable reason for using them.

- **Overreach boots**, designed to protect the horse if he strikes the heel area of a front foot, should be used with caution. Some trainers believe overreach boots should not be used when jumping or working at speed because if the horse treads on the bottom of the boot, he may trip and fall. If the boots are too big or too long this can definitely happen.

A horse who overreaches when ridden will often improve as his schooling progresses and he becomes more balanced. Your vet and farrier may also have some suggestions.

- **Tendon boots** should protect the vulnerable tendon area against impact. Research shows they are unlikely to provide support, though some designs are claimed to do so.
- **Travel boots** designed for use in transport vary in design and must fit properly. If they are too large and slip down the leg, the horse is likely to be irritated or even frightened and will stamp or slip. However, well-designed boots which stay in place and cover from the knees or hocks to the heels are very useful.

You will also find specialist designs, such as **polo boots**—heavy duty boots to protect against accidental blows—and **over-the-hoof boots** meant to be used in place of a shoe.

Leg bandages may be used to give support when working, protect the horse when travelling and provide support and/or warmth in the stable.

Exercise bandages made from stretch material and designed to be applied over padding are rarely used now. Some riders use close-fitting training boots or schooling leg wraps designed to be used without padding, but they must have a purpose and be correctly adjusted. Don't use something just to follow the example of a rider you admire!

Stable and travelling bandages are wider, thicker and less stretchy than exercise ones. They must always be used over suitable padding, which can range from cotton or felt-type pads to gel pads. Bandaging guidelines are:

1. Start with the bandage rolled correctly, so that you finish with the fastenings on the outside.
2. Bandage from front to back to avoid pressure on tendons and ligaments.
3. Keep pressure even as you bandage down, then back up the leg.
4. Tapes or ties should be fastened on the outside of the leg, on the side—not on the back, where they could put pressure on the tendons, or at the front, where they could press on the cannon bones.

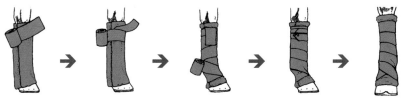

Stable and travelling bandages (above) are wider, thicker and less stretchy than exercise ones.

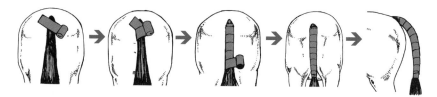

Elasticated tail bandages are used to protect the hair when travelling and to keep a shaped or pulled tail neat. You can use a tailguard as well as or instead of a bandage if you prefer, though these won't always fit horses with fat docks and/or thick tails.

To put on a tail bandage:

- Roll it the right way round with the tapes or fastening strap inside.
- Dampen the hair, but NOT the bandage. Bandages shrink and will pull too tight as they dry.
- Stand behind but slightly to one side of the horse so you can't get kicked.
- Unroll about 20cm (8in) and place it across the top of the tail. Hold this section in your left hand and the bandage roll in your right.
- Make your first turn, fold over the spare end and bandage over it.
- Bandage down to just below the end of the tail bones (dock), keeping the tension even.
- Tie or fasten, keeping the same tension as the bandage. With smaller ponies, you may need to bandage partway back up the tail before fastening. Some people prefer to do this as standard.
- Gently bend the tail into a comfortable position.
- To remove a tail bandage, undo the tapes or fastenings, grasp the bandage at the top of the tail with both hands and slide down and off.

Rug Rules

There are so many types of rug available and so many high-tech materials that a horse could easily have a clothing collection larger than his owner's. The main types are:

- *Turnout rugs*, used as outdoor protection in bad weather.
- *Stable rugs*, used to keep a horse warm in the stable. Some owners find it easier to use multipurpose rugs than traditional non-waterproof stable rugs. This can save time and money—though rugs must still be checked and adjusted twice a day—but the disadvantages are that although a rug with a wet and/or muddy outer layer will dry on the horse, it will spread dirt as it dries.

- *Summer sheets*, traditionally made from cotton and used to keep a horse clean and protect him from flies and light draughts.
- *Coolers*, which have replaced old-fashioned anti-sweat rugs and are used to dry off a wet or sweating horse.
- *Thermal rugs*, made from special lightweight fabrics which keep the horse warm and transfer moisture from his body to outside of the rug.
- *Fly rugs*, which form a barrier against insects. Fly masks protect the vulnerable eye area, but must fit well.
- *Sweet itch rugs/stretch body covers*, which act as a barrier against the biting midge Culicoides (*see* Chapter 6.)
- *Exercise rugs* (quarter sheets), which are used to keep a clipped horse warm when riding slow work or warming up. Designs which fit round the saddle rather than being placed underneath it are often easier to manage and more versatile.

Your first decision is whether or not he needs to wear a particular rug. Will it improve his comfort and well-being or would he be better off without it? Ponies with very thick winter coats, such as Exmoors and Shetlands, have a great natural weather-beating system and if they have good forage and shelter and don't need to be clipped, will often be better off unrugged. However, an old pony who struggles to keep weight on or a clipped animal will need rugging. (Chapter 9 gives more advice on clipping.)

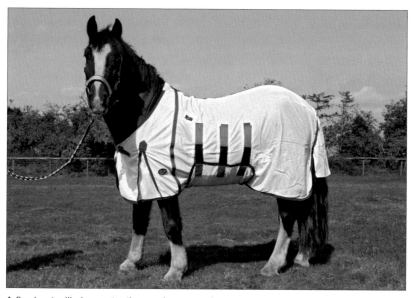

A fly sheet will give protection against many insects.

Fit for the Job

Rugs only work if they stay in place, so must be the right size. They are usually measured from the centre of the chest to the rear of the quarters, and sized in 3-inch increments—rug manufacturers haven't gone metric! Ideally, a rug with a standard neck should lie 5–10cm (2–4in) in front of the withers and finish at the top of the tail.

Exercise rugs are measured either along the centre back line or sold in small, medium and large sizes.

A chest expander can solve the problem of a horse who is wide across the chest but on whom a bigger rug would slip.

Don't assume that the taller the horse, the bigger the rug he will need. A 13.2hh with a wide chest and deep body may need the same size as a narrower but much taller horse.

The rug should be deep enough to cover his body and shaped to allow freedom of movement. A rug which is too small will rub and cause pressure points, but so will one which is too large, as it will slide back. White hairs in the wither area are usually a sign that a horse has worn a rug which pulled down and caused pressure.

Rugs are usually designed on the basis that the wearer will have average proportions, but as horses, like people, aren't made from the same mould, you may have to shop around for a make that suits your horse best.

The commonest problem is that of the horse with a chest relatively wide for his height and length. Many cobs and native ponies come into this category and if you try a rug which fits at the chest, it will often be too deep in the neck and will slip back and apply pressure. A chest expander can solve this problem.

Neck covers on turnout rugs, either built-in or separate, help keep a horse warm and dry. They must not rub or restrict him whilst he's grazing.

Many designs have tail flaps for extra protection. Check that the horse can lift his tail easily.

Adjust to Fit

Rugs are usually secured by T-bars or buckles at the centre chest and by cross-surcingles. Some manufactures use different methods, such as under-belly harnesses; to adjust these, follow the makers' instructions.

You should be able to fit a hand's width between the front of the rug and the horse's chest. Cross-surcingles should cross in the centre of the horse's belly and be fastened to allow a hand's width between them and the horse's body.

Some designs have legstraps, though they have become less popular. Rear legstraps are usually linked and front legstraps left unlinked, but follow the manufacturer's instructions.

Keep it Clean

All equipment must be kept clean and checked frequently to make sure it is safe and in good condition. Dirty tack, boots, numnahs or rugs can cause discomfort and skin infections.

You'll learn at rallies how to clean tack, but here are some guidelines:

- Wash your horse's bit every time you remove his bridle to prevent the bit becoming crusted with dried saliva and food particles. If tack gets wet or muddy, dry slowly at room temperature—not in front of a heater, or it may become brittle. Wash off mud quickly, blot excess water and dry.

- Wipe off dirt and grease every time you ride. At least once a week, dismantle tack and clean thoroughly. Use a conditioning product regularly: follow the manufacturer's instructions on application and frequency of use. When your tack is dismantled, check stitching and leather for wear and damage.

- Washable rugs and girths can be washed in a domestic machine, or rugs can be taken to a specialist rug-wash company. Tie girths in an old pillow case or use special washing bags to prevent buckles causing damage.

- Synthetic tack and boots should be cleaned according to the manufacturer's instructions.

Adjust cross-surcingles so they cross in the centre of the body and allow you to fit a hand between them and the horse.

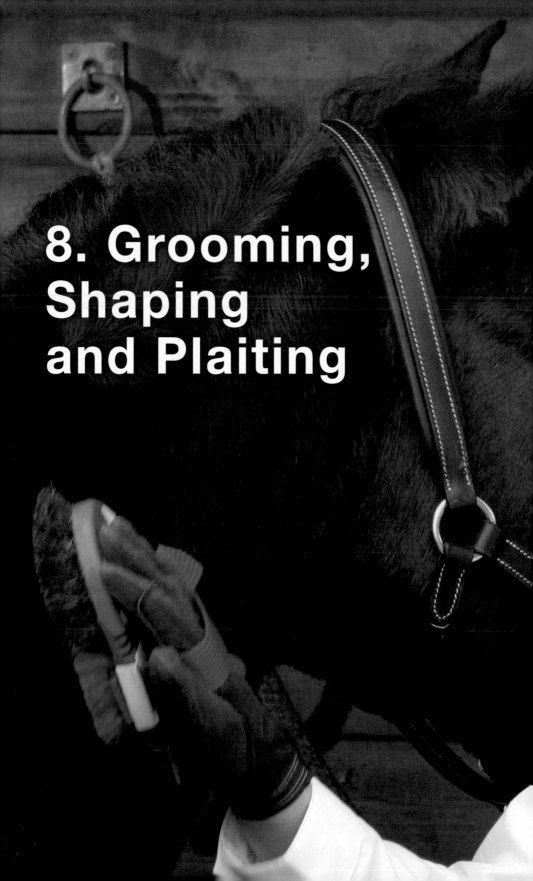

8. Grooming, Shaping and Plaiting

There is more to grooming than just keeping a horse looking smart. It's also a time to assess how he's feeling and spot minor injuries. Never underestimate the value of hands-on time with your horse!

On large yards, horses are often tied up in their stables to be groomed, because this is safer than having lots of horses being brought in and out of their boxes at the same time. However, when possible, tie up your horse outside to groom him. This way, you don't spread dust and dirt in the stable environment.

Basic grooming techniques apply to all horses and ponies, but the equipment you use and the routine you follow should be adapted to his lifestyle. A thick-coated animal who lives out unrugged needs the weather-proofing qualities of the natural grease in his coat, whilst a horse who is stabled part of the time, rugged and clipped when necessary can be groomed more thoroughly.

Be considerate: a pony with a thick coat probably won't object if you use a stiff-bristled brush to remove dried mud, but a thin-skinned or clipped one won't like it. Be patient with animals who object to being groomed; they may associate it with previous discomfort. Adapt your techniques, stay safe by wearing a hard hat and being careful where you stand to minimise the risk of kicks and make sure the horse is tied up 'short' so he can't swing his head round and bite.

Clever Kit

With experience, you'll add favourite tools to your grooming kit. A basic kit should comprise:

- *Hoofpick* for removing mud and stones and checking whether shoes are secure.
- *Rubber curry comb or plastic groomer* for removing dried mud and loose hair and lifting grease to the surface of the coat.
- *Whisk or flick dandy brush*—a brush with long, flexible bristles to flick dust and dirt away from the coat.
- *Body brush* with short bristles to remove dust and grease and massage the skin. Can also be used on manes and tails.
- *Metal curry comb* for cleaning a body brush. It's easier to tap dirt out of a metal curry comb than a rubber one.
- *Cotton wool or cotton pads* to provide a hygienic way of cleaning eyes, nose, mouth and dock. This is more hygienic than using

You will soon find items to add to the essentials in your grooming kit.

sponges, as you can use and then discard a separate piece or pad for each area. This minimises the risk of infection—if, for instance, you use the same sponge for each eye you can spread a problem from one area to another.

- *Stiff-bristled dandy brush*—only for use on thick coats and only when horses don't object.
- *Sweat scraper* for removing excess water after bathing or washing down.
- *Fly repellent.*

85

Extras

If you get the chance, see what professional grooms include in their kit. You might find:

- *Hairbrush with widely spaced bristles*. When used correctly, this separates mane and tail hairs without breaking them.
- *Stable rubber or grooming mitten* to give a final wipe over.
- *Cactus cloth*, made from coarsely woven fabric to remove dried sweat and light stains.
- *Trimming scissors* with curved, rounded ends.
- *Pulling comb* with short teeth to thin or shape manes and tails. (*See* the section on shaping up later in this chapter.)
- *Shaping combs*, which offer a kinder and safer way of shaping tails than traditional pulling technique and give a smart result.
- Small, soft-bristled *facial brush.*
- *Hoof dressing.* Ask your farrier's advice about products intended to make your horse look smarter when competing, as you don't want to use anything which will dry out the hoof horn.

There are useful products which make life easier, such as mane and tail detangling sprays, but nothing beats a thorough, proper groom!

Everyday Essentials

There are a few jobs which should be carried out daily whether or not the horse is being ridden.

Pick out his feet, check that shoes are secure and that there are no risen clenches. A farrier clenches up a shoe by turning over and twisting off the nail end. What's left is called a clench and if you get a risen clench, the shoe will be less secure and the protruding metal could cause injury to the opposite leg.

To lift a horse's leg, run your hand down it to the fetlock and apply gentle pressure. Start at the shoulder or hindquarters to give him warning. A well-mannered horse will lift his leg easily, but if you have problems, ask for advice.

Lift the foot just high enough to

When picking out a foot, be careful not to dig into the sensitive V-shaped frog.

allow you to work and hold the foot at the toe to put less strain on your arm. Use your hoofpick from heel to toe and avoid digging into the sensitive frog (the V-shaped cleft). Put the foot down rather than drop it, which will give the pony more confidence in you.

Brush off a horse before riding to remove dried mud and dirt, especially on areas where tack will touch. The traditional way of brushing off a stabled, rugged horse is called quartering, because you can deal with a quarter at a time and still keep the horse warm.

Unfasten and fold back the front half of the rug and brush over his front half. Then fold the back half of the rug towards the font and deal with the rear half, finishing by tidying his mane and tail.

Groomed to Perfection

Ideally, all horses *except* those living out all the time should be groomed thoroughly once a day. The best time to groom is after exercise, as the horse will be warm and the pores of his skin will be open. If necessary, put a rug on him so he doesn't catch a chill and adjust it as above.

Many owners build their own grooming routines, but the following method works well and means you aren't transferring dirt from one part of a horse to another. Work on one side, then the other.

1. Run your hands over the horse to check for any problems.
2. Pick out his feet and check shoes.
3. Separate mane hair with your fingers. Push the mane over the neck and brush through, then flip the hair back and repeat on the top side.
4. Starting at the neck, use a rubber curry comb or groomer in a circular motion (as pictured below). Hold it in the hand nearest to the horse for maximum efficiency. You may be able to omit this step with a clipped or fine-coated horse, though most enjoy the massaging effect.
5. Work from top to bottom as you move along the horse, but avoid any areas where he shows extra sensitivity, such as the belly.
6. Flick off dirt with a flick dandy brush.
7. Separate tail hair with your fingers and if necessary, brush it out with a body brush or hairbrush. Hold the

Use a rubber curry comb or groomer in a circular motion to raise dust and dirt to the surface of the coat.

tail near the ends and brush the bottom section, then gradually move up. Brushing downwards to the ends each time avoids creating tangles.

Move a body brush over a metal curry comb in this direction to remove dirt and grease.

8. Standing with your feet slightly apart and the body brush in the hand nearest to the horse, brush in short strokes from neck to tail. Lean into the brush to put your weight behind each stroke without straining your arms. After every few strokes, clean the brush by running it over your curry comb. Follow the direction pictured above so you don't cover yourself with dirt. Tap the curry comb on the ground to expel dirt.

9. Clean the horse's face gently with a body brush or small facial brush.

10. Clean each eye and nostril with separate pads and use another pad to clean the dock area.

11. Wipe over with a lightly dampened cloth to remove any dust on the coat surface.

12. Apply fly repellent and/or hoof dressing if needed.

Strapping

Grooming will clean your horse and have a massaging effect, but strapping goes that bit farther. This technique helps stimulate circulation and builds muscles by making them contract and relax.

Traditionally, grooms strapped with a wisp, which was made from twisting hay to make a rope and looping it into a pad. Today, most people prefer to use a leather strapping pad.

Work on the neck, topline and shoulder, but not on the legs, belly or loins. Bring the pad down firmly, wait for the muscle to tense and, as it relaxes, repeat. Start with a mild impact and gradually build up, but judge the pressure you apply according to your horse's reaction.

A leather strapping pad is the modern equivalent of the traditional hay wisp.

Strap after grooming, when the horse is warm and relaxed. As a guide, build up on each side to 100 strapping strokes on the neck, 50 on the shoulder, 100 on the quarters and 25 on the second thigh. Alter the ratio if you want to improve a particular area.

Bathing

There will be times when you need to bath a horse, but only do so when there is no risk of him getting a chill. In general, it is not recommended that you bath a horse who lives out unrugged, as this will remove the protective grease in his coat, or who has a full winter coat, as it will take a long time for him to dry even if you use a thermal rug.

However, you should be able to wash manes and tails without causing problems and you can sponge off stains. Always use shampoo formulated for horses—not washing-up liquid or washing powder, as this may cause a skin reaction—and always rinse thoroughly.

There is also a technique called hot cloth washing, often used in racing stables, which can be useful. To do this, you need two buckets of hand-hot water to which small amounts of shampoo have been added and pieces of towelling or other suitable material. Soak a piece of towelling in one bucket and wring out. Use the hot cloth in a circular motion against the lie of the coat to remove dust and dirt. Rinse the cloth in the second bucket as often as you need to keep it clean. When you've finished, towel dry and use a rug which transfers moisture to the outside layer.

If your horse sweats in areas where tack has rested, sponge or wash him down to remove and use a sweat scraper and clean towel to remove as much moisture as possible. Use a thermal rug or cooler to speed the drying process if necessary.

You can wash a mane or tail without giving a horse a full bath.

Shaping Manes and Tails

There will be times when you need to shorten and perhaps thin your horse's mane and tail. If you have a purebred native or a purebred Arab and want to show him, check breed society and showing organisation guidelines. The same applies if you have a cob and wish to show him with a full mane, tail and feathers (leg hair).

The traditional way of shaping and thinning manes and tails is to pull them with a pulling comb. Some horses don't mind this, but it should always be done after exercise when they are warm, the skin pores are open and hairs come out more easily. Pull out *only a few hairs* at a time.

Be particularly careful if you pull a tail. Some horses don't mind, but you should still stand to the side, not directly behind. Take hairs from the side and, keeping both sides even, work to halfway down the dock.

Other horses find this uncomfortable or even painful and may kick. It's unfair and potentially dangerous to try and pull hair in these cases. Instead, use a shaping comb/rake or a thinning blade on manes and tails. Some owners prefer this method as standard practice. The easiest way to learn how to get good results is to watch someone who does it well! You will probably want to level the bottom of your horse's tail. Choose a length appropriate to his breed or type. Watch him led out in hand to see how he carries his tail naturally and before you cut, ask a helper to place a hand gently under his dock to approximate that.

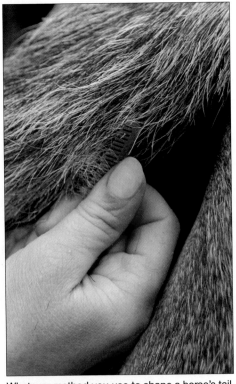

Whatever method you use to shape a horse's tail, be considerate of his comfort and be aware of your safety.

Perfect Plaits

You need to make sure your horse's mane is the same thickness and length all the way down the neck before you plait. It's easiest if it is about 10–15cm (4-6in) long, but thickness is more influential. It's easier to plait a thinner mane than a thicker one.

Convention says there should be an odd number of plaits down the neck plus one for the forelock. Experiment to see how many plaits look best on your horse and remember, practice makes perfect.

To get a neat, professional look, secure your plaits with a needle and thread. If you are in a hurry or practising, use rubber bands.

If you want the top of your horse's tail to look neat, but prefer to leave the hair long, plait it. Take a small section of hair from each side of the top of the tail and a third from the centre. Plait down, taking in a small section of hair each time each time you cross a side section over a centre one.

Stitching plaits makes for a neater and more secure result but you can use rubber bands when practising or if you are in a hurry.

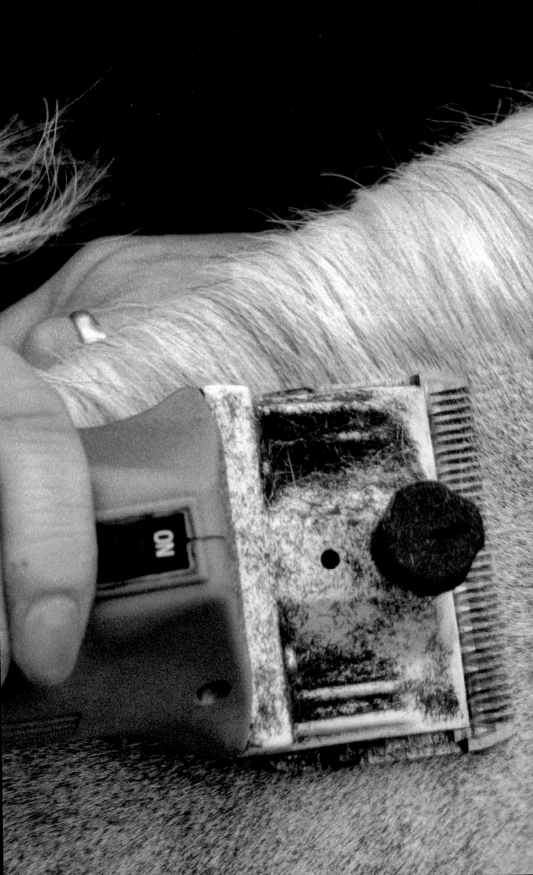

9. Clipping

The main reason for clipping a horse is to keep him comfortable. If the level of his work means he sweats excessively because of a thick coat, he will be happier and healthier if you take some of it off. There may be times when you need to clip a horse who is not in work: in particular, one with Cushing's syndrome who grows a thick coat all year round.

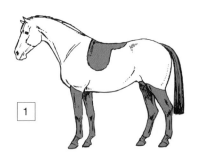

A clipped horse will look smart, but look on this as a bonus rather than as your main objective! The best way to learn how to clip is to watch someone experienced and competent, then try clipping a quiet, experienced animal under their supervision. Inexperienced or nervous animals should only be clipped by experienced people who can be guaranteed to handle them safely, calmly and fairly.

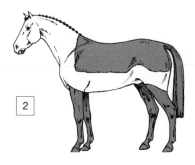

There are different types of clip to suit different horses and their lifestyles. They can be adapted to suit your horse; for instance, a trace or blanket clip can be high or low. Only remove as much hair as is necessary.

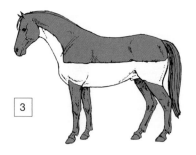

Traditionally, horses were not clipped until they had full winter coats and the last clip was made before the summer coat came through. Now, it's acceptable to clip whenever a horse's comfort dictates.

If your horse is freeze-marked for security, clip the area when necessary so it can be read clearly, even if you leave the rest of him unclipped.

Types of clip: (1) Hunter; (2) Blanket; (3) Trace; (4) Belly and gullet. (Gold= hair on, White = clipped areas.)

Which Clip?

- A *bib clip*, where hair is clipped from the throat and chest, is great for animals in light work.
- A *belly and gullet clip* extends the clipped area of a bib clip along the belly.
- A *trace clip*, originally used on driving horses, gets its name because it follows the lines of the traces in a driving harness.
- A *blanket clip* leaves a blanket-shaped area of hair and is suitable for most horses.
- A *chaser clip* leaves hair on the top half of the neck and the hindquarters, extending in a diagonal line from the ears to the stifle.
- A *hunter clip* leaves hair on the legs and in the shape of a saddle patch. It is only suitable for horses who are in hard work.
- A *full clip* removes all hair and so leaves vulnerable leg and back areas without protection.

Safety First

The area where you clip your horse must be dry and light and the horse should be clean, dry and relaxed. Put a tail bandage on him to keep tail hair out of the way. If you clip in a stable, lift all bedding and pile it at the sides, so clipped hair can be swept up. Take out water and feed containers or cover automatic waterers.

If your yard is quiet and safe, your horse is good to clip and the weather is dry and still, you can clip outside his stable. Never clip outside when it is windy or raining or when things may happen on the yard which will excite or worry your horse.

The person clipping the horse needs a helper, to reassure an inexperienced horse and help if the area around the elbows is clipped (*see* later in this section). Both clipper and helper should wear a hard hat; a horse can injure you if he throws up his head, strikes out or cow kicks. You hope accidents won't happen, but it's better to take preventive measures.

Wear suitable rubber-soled footwear and tie back long hair. Overalls will protect your clothes.

You *must* have some kind of circuit-breaking mechanism and must be careful to keep the clipper cable away from a horse's feet and legs. Make sure the cable doesn't touch him accidentally as you manoeuvre the clippers, as this may startle him.

Choosing Clippers

There are different types of clippers for different purposes. Battery-operated ones are usually quieter than electric ones, which can help when clipping nervous or inexperienced horses. However, not all designs are suitable for anything more than minimal clips. If you don't have an electricity supply, you can find clippers which run off car batteries.

Fine or medium clipper blades are best for most scenarios. Blades must be kept sharp and will need to be re-sharpened at intervals by a specialist. Never use blunt blades, which will pull at the coat and cause discomfort instead of cutting cleanly through the hair.

Blades must be lubricated before you start and at intervals throughout the clipping process. Use only special clipper oil.

Ready to Clip

Read the manufacturers' instructions and make sure the blade tension is correct. Make sure you have everything you need—including a rug to keep your horse warm if you are taking off anything but a minimal amount of hair.

Never clip when you're in a hurry and always be quiet, calm and patient.

Mark out clipping lines with a dampened chalk stick. At places where the line on one side meets the line on the other, such as over the withers, use a piece of string to make sure both sides join up.

Clipping Techniques

Always talk to the horse and run the clippers before you start, so he accepts the noise. This applies to experienced horses as well as inexperienced ones: don't take anything for granted, especially if it's the first clip of the year.

Start clipping on a less sensitive area: if possible, the shoulder. If you're not taking hair from the shoulder area, start on the underside of the neck.

Before you make the first cut, put your hand on the area you will start work on and rest the running clippers on top. This minimises the vibration but gives a hint of what is to come. If the horse is happy, rest the clippers on the horse before starting to clip; if he's worried, spend time getting him used to the noise and sensation.

If you're new to clipping and your horse remains worried, don't get yourself into a difficult or potentially dangerous situation. It's better to get help than to push yourself and your horse too far.

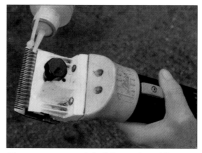

Always use special oil formulated for use with clippers.

Clip against the lie of the coat, keeping pressure firm and even and holding the blades flat against the coat when clipping large areas. Overlap each stroke with the next to avoid leaving lines and if necessary, angle the clipper blades when clipping fiddly bits.

Mark out your clipping lines with dampened chalk.

You lose heat if you take off your coat. So does your horse, so keep a rug handy to fold and place over the unclipped half of his body whilst you work on the other half. Lightweight, thermal rugs are particularly useful here.

As you clip, stop at intervals to clean and oil the blades, check that they are not hot and that air vents are clear. If the sound of the motor changes to signify that the clippers are running more slowly, stop immediately and do the same.

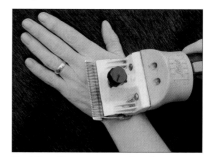

Rest the clippers on your hand to minimise vibration and accustom the horse to the idea of being clipped.

A Bit at a Time

Different areas present their own clipping challenges. Here are some ideas to help you perfect your technique and make the most of your horse. If necessary, check breed or type guidelines first with the relevant society.

- If you're clipping his neck, take the blades as near the mane as you can, but don't clip into the mane hairs. If you do, you'll get short, spiky re-growth for some time.

- Don't clip hair from the inside of his ears: he needs it for protection against insects and foreign bodies such as hay seeds. If he's amenable, close his ear gently with one hand and neaten the edges, using trimming clippers if you have them. If he doesn't like clippers on his ears, use trimming scissors instead.

- An expert can clip out a horse's head, but an easier way is to clip up to where the bridle cheeks rest. Use chalk and a piece of string to mark out an ear-to-mouth line.

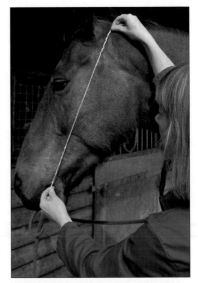

Use string and chalk again to mark a line from the base of the ears to the lips.

- Some people trim off whiskers to give a smart appearance, but others prefer to leave them to act as a sensory aid.

- The clip at the top of the foreleg should form an upside-down V, following the line of the muscles. Follow the muscle line for the hindlegs, too.

- Hair spirals outwards from the stifle. Turn the clippers to follow this.

- When you clip around the girth and elbow areas, get your helper to lift the front leg and stretch it gently forwards. This means there are fewer wrinkles and less chance of the horse being nicked.

- If you trim your horse's legs, clip against the lie of the coat for a close finish but trim in the direction of coat growth for a more natural look. Be careful: some horses don't like clippers against their legs at first, so, as before, place your hand against the horse and hold the clippers on top to start with and when he's happy, hold them against the leg itself.

- If he fidgets when having a front leg held, ask your helper to pick up the other foreleg. If he dislikes having a hindleg clipped, your helper should pick up the foreleg on the same side. For instance, if he is restless when his near hind is clipped, ask your helper to pick up his near fore.

- However, don't take risks. If necessary, use scissors and a comb to

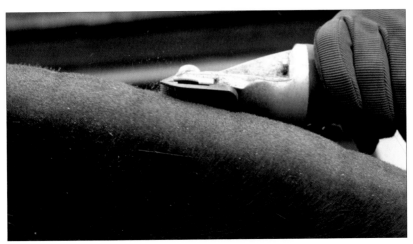

Hog a mane in three stages, first running the clippers up the centre and then up each side.

trim his fetlocks. Hold the comb against the leg and trim the hair which comes through the teeth. Keep changing the angle of the comb to avoid making 'steps.'

- Trimming techniques can make an unclipped horse look smarter. Tidy his jaw and leg areas and, by creating a sharper outline, you'll give a woolly horse a new look.

Hogging a Mane

Cobs (and polo ponies) often have hogged manes. In the case of cobs, this is to show off their powerful necks. Polo ponies are hogged to prevent the mallet becoming tangled in mane hair.

Hog a mane in three stages. First, clip up the centre, then clip up each side. If you are hogging a long mane, clipping or cutting off much of the long hair first makes it easier. It takes anything from six months to a year for a hogged mane and forelock to grow out completely.

Remember...

A horse who has just been clipped will usually be lively, as he will be more sensitive to wind and temperature. Be prepared for him to seem bright or even to throw a buck! If you have taken off most of his coat, he may need an exercise rug for slow work or when warming up for harder work.

**10.
Transport
and Care
Away from
Home**

By now, you will know how to keep your horse happy, healthy and safe at home. You also need to know how to look after him during transport and whilst you're away from home—perhaps at a Pony Club rally or competition.

Anyone driving a horsebox (lorry) or towing a trailer must understand the legislation covering horse transport. This includes classes of horsebox and who is permitted to drive them; weight restrictions; the difference between private and commercial use and whether a driver must pass a trailer-towing test. If you tow a trailer, make sure your vehicle is capable of doing it.

It is a complicated subject, but must be understood to avoid breaking the law and potentially incurring heavy penalties. Government websites such as the ones below are a good place to find information:

- Driver and Vehicle Licensing Agency *www.dvla.gov.uk*
- Vehicle and Operator Services Agency *www.vosa.gov.uk*
- Dept. of Environment, Food and Rural Affairs *www.defra.gov.uk*

The law states that whenever you travel your horse, however short the journey, you must have his passport with you.

Preparation and driving techniques are the key to giving your horse a good journey. Always allow plenty of time and get all your tack, equipment and any hay and feed supplies ready the day before. Add a container of water just before you leave so it stays as fresh as possible.

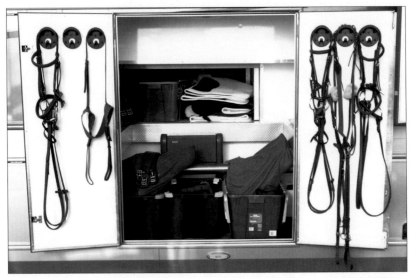

Make a list of all the things you will need to take in your horsebox or towing vehicle.

No matter how experienced you are, it's a good idea to list what you need to take. Grooms who work for top riders often have checklists for each horse, because it's too easy to forget a small but important item. For security reasons, it's best not to leave your vehicle full of expensive gear overnight.

If you need to plait your horse's mane and tail, either do so the night before or allow extra time on the day. Professional grooms can plait a mane in 20 minutes, but that takes a lot of practice! If you feed overnight hay from a net, leaving the forelock plait until morning will minimise the number of seeds and short pieces getting caught in the hair.

A poll guard can be used for extra protection.

Another trick is to cut a leg from a pair of old tights, lay this along the top of the neck and over the plaits and fasten a plaiting band round each plait. The material is stretchy, so won't pull taut when your horse lowers his head.

Travel Kit

Protect your horse when travelling with:
- A comfortable, well-fitting headcollar. Leather is safest. It will break if there is an emergency and the horse gets caught up, but nylon may not and can result in injury even when the headcollar rope is tied to a breakable loop.
- If your horse tends to throw up his head, check he is comfortable in his travelling position and, as a safeguard, use a poll guard to protect this vulnerable area.
- Boots or bandages.
- A tail bandage and/or tailguard
- A rug or lightweight sheet appropriate for the conditions. Take spare rugs of different weights to account for a change in temperature.

Stay Safe

Horseboxes, trailers and towing vehicles must be safe and legal. Make pre-drive checks before every journey and walk round before you drive off to make sure everything is in order. You could cause serious damage if, for instance, you forget to raise the fold-down steps on your horsebox.

Maintaining horseboxes, towing vehicles and trailers is beyond the scope of this book. However, it's a vital area to keep you, other road users and your horse safe, so make sure you know what you can and must do and when you need to call on an expert.

Compared to a horsebox, a trailer is mechanically simple. However, it still needs to be checked before every trip and maintained and serviced regularly.

Read your trailer manual. This will give you vital information such as correct tyre pressures, which are often much higher than those for the average car and must be checked before every trip.

The tyres on both your car and trailer, including spares, must have a good tread. The legal minimum is 1.6mm ($^1/_{16}$ in) over the central 75 per cent of their width for the whole circumference, but this offers little grip on wet roads and anything under 3mm ($^1/_8$ in) may be inadequate.

The tyre walls must be in good condition with no deep cuts or bulges. Punctures can still happen, so it's a good idea to carry a special wedge-shaped trailer lift.

This sort of design is safer than a conventional jack, because when horses move around it is less likely that the trailer will be rocked off. They are easy to use: the wheel to be replaced is lifted off the ground by towing its partner on the same side on to a recess on top of the wedge.

Don't forget to make last minute checks before leaving to ensure you haven't, for instance, forgotten to raise fold-up steps.

Check tyres on towing cars and horseboxes regularly.

The car's towball should be greased and every time you hitch up, you should make sure that the trailer lights are working properly and that the lamp lenses are clean and undamaged. The breakaway cable, which is a legal requirement on a braked trailer, must be in good condition and not attached to anything on the car that may be pulled off.

Simple but important maintenance includes cleaning out the trailer *every time it's used*, lifting and cleaning under rubber matting regularly and checking all hinges and locks. Your trailer should be serviced and checked regularly by a recognised dealer.

Loading and Unloading

A horse who is used to travelling and has been transported considerately should load easily. If you have problems, get expert help. Tips for safe and easy loading include:

- Always wear a hard hat, gloves and sensible footwear.
- Allow plenty of time and stay calm.
- Using a snaffle bridle (minus the noseband) over the headcollar your horse will travel in will give you more control.
- Park the horsebox or trailer so the interior is light and inviting and your horse has safe footing.
- Present him straight at the ramp, not at an angle.
- Stay beside him and look ahead, not back at him.
- Always approach the ramp in walk and let him take his time. Don't scold him for pawing the ramp: he is testing his footing.
- Never stand directly behind a ramp when raising or lowering it.
- If you have to tie up a horse outside the vehicle, tie the lead rope to a breakable loop.
- Never leave horses unattended, whether they are on the vehicle or tied to it.

Park the horsebox or trailer so the interior is light and inviting and present your horse straight at the ramp.

Drive Time

Safe, considerate driving gives your horse a better journey. Whether you drive a lorry or tow a trailer, remember the following:

- If you are legally entitled to drive a horsebox but have never driven anything bigger than a car, consider taking lessons from a qualified, specialist instructor. It's foolhardy to load up a horse and drive off, even if the law says you can.
- There are also qualified instructors who can teach you to tow safely. Again, it isn't safe to load up and go. You should at least practise in a safe, off-road environment and should make your first road trips towing an empty trailer. Many people find reversing a trailer is challenging, so practise this off-road, too.
- Other road users may not appreciate the extra room a large vehicle or towing set-up takes or needs. You need to think ahead and, unfortunately, be prepared for other drivers to do stupid things such as cutting in front of you.
- When you make your first driving or towing trips with a horse on board, you will notice the effect of the extra weight—and the fact that it moves! Brake and change gear smoothly and in plenty of time, corner and negotiate roundabouts slowly and remember that restricted vision means you must rely on your side mirrors much more than when driving a car.

Negotiate corners and roundabouts slowly.

At a Show

When you arrive, check that your horse is comfortable. Take him off the vehicle as soon as possible and if he has to stand even for a few minutes, lower the ramp to allow air to circulate and offer him a drink. Some horses may be too interested in what is going on to drink at first, so if he refuses, offer him water when he has settled.

Unloading him as soon as possible means you can check him over and make sure he isn't too hot. Do this before you look round a showground or look for a secretary's tent: a horse can soon overheat when left standing, especially in hot weather.

Don't use your horse as a grandstand whilst you watch other people. If you're not warming up or working/competing, stay off his back. On hot days, use any shady areas available.

When you've finished competing or working him, walk him round to cool down before putting on his travel gear to go home. If necessary, use a cooler or thermal rug on to prevent him catching a chill.

In hot weather—and especially in hot, humid conditions—experts now advise alternate washing and walking.

You will have restricted vision compared with driving a car so must rely on side mirrors.

Back Home

When you get home, check your horse over. Wash off any mud if you weren't able to do so before you left, and feel as well as look for any injuries or areas of heat or swelling which need first aid or veterinary assessment.

A stabled horse can be left to settle with a haynet and, if appropriate, his normal feed. It used to be thought that a horse should be given a bran mash after hard work or competition, but this advice no longer applies. Giving a bran mash as a one-off breaks the feeding rule of making all changes gradually and can cause rather than prevent digestive upset.

The horse who lives out should be turned out as usual, if necessary wearing a breathable rug, so that he can walk round, have a roll and graze.

Whether he lives in or out, check him when he has had time to settle and check again later on. If you keep him on a livery yard, ask the owner to check him for you. It's important to check that he hasn't 'broken out'—started sweating—which could cause him to catch a chill.

If he has, he should be walked until he is dry and warm; an appropriate cooler or thermal rug may help with this. A vigorous rub with dry towels will help start the drying process if your horse has a particularly thick coat.

Next Day

Check him first thing next day, again looking for signs of injury, heat or swelling. If he seems happy, walk and trot him in hand to make sure he isn't stiff or, despite your care, lame.

Travelling is tiring, so it's usually best to give your horse a day off after a show or Pony Club rally. Turn him out so he can keep moving.

Last Word

You never stop learning about how to care for a horse. They all share the same basic physical characteristics and instincts, but every animal is still an individual.

One reason is that horses, like us, are shaped by previous experiences. Another is that the way you look after and ride a horse affects his behaviour and well-being. Feeding is an obvious example: a horse who is fed too much high energy food and not given enough time in the field is likely to be more 'difficult' than one whose owner manages him correctly.

This book and other Pony Club publications will give you a framework, and experts such as your vet and farrier should provide back-up. Your role is to be a conscientious, thinking owner: ideas sometimes change, especially in veterinary matters, and we sometimes have to update the way we do things. At the same time, new is not always better and you have to decide whether or not you agree with a particular philosophy.

Your horse will be an important part of your life and you will probably think of him as a friend. We all become fond of our horses, but the way to show we care for them is to remember that they are horses—not people with four legs, however much character they have!

As a Member of The Pony Club, you can follow a structured training path that will help you ride and care for your horse as well as you possibly can. Make the most of that opportunity, learn as much as you can from qualified experts in specialist fields and you will know you are doing your best for your horse.

Index